D0036511

media

MANUAL

studio television production and directing

MANUAL

studio television production and directing

andrew h. utterback

ELSEVIER

AMSTERDAM • BOSTON • HEIDELBERG • LONDON
NEW YORK • OXFORD • PARIS • SAN DIEGO
SAN FRANCISCO • SINGAPORE • SYDNEY • TOKYO
Focal Press is an imprint of Elsevier

Focal
Press

Acquisitions Editor:	Elinor Actipis
Publishing Services Manager:	George Morrison
Senior Project Manager:	Brandy Lilly
Assistant Editor:	Robin Weston
Marketing Manager:	Christine Degon Veroulis
Cover Design:	Eric DeCicco

Focal Press is an imprint of Elsevier
30 Corporate Drive, Suite 400, Burlington, MA 01803, USA
Linacre House, Jordan Hill, Oxford OX2 8DP, UK

Recognizing the importance of preserving what has been written, Elsevier prints its books on acid-free paper whenever possible.

Library of Congress Cataloging-in-Publication Data
Application submitted.

British Library Cataloguing-in-Publication Data
A catalogue record for this book is available from the British Library.

ISBN 13: 978-0-240-80873-4
ISBN 10: 0-240-80873-8

For information on all Focal Press publications
visit our website at www.books.elsevier.com

Working together to grow
libraries in developing countries

www.elsevier.com | www.bookaid.org | www.sabre.org

ELSEVIER   BOOK AID International   Sabre Foundation

Transferred to Digital Printing in 2011

Contents

ASSISTANT DIRECTING AND DIRECTING

For

Elias, Anna, and Myles,

Susanna,

and Mom and Dad

Acknowledgments

Time given to a writing project takes time and attention away from people close to the author. I am indebted to my wife Susanna for her patience. I owe my son Elias sand-castles too numerous to count. A great deal of what I know about television production I learned on the job from Wayne M. Nesbitt. I would like to thank Alex Pikas, Fred Lazlo, Joe Young II, John Jennings, and a few other notable Production Technicians who, in the fine State of Maryland, taught me the finer details of studio production.

My uncle, Roger Hicks, deserves recognition for answering many of my television questions over the years and for helping bring PBS to the State of Wyoming at KCWC, Lander-Riverton.

A great deal of what I know about teaching I learned from observing and copying my Professors at Eastern New Mexico University and the University of Utah. James A. Anderson, Tim Ashmore, Robert K. Avery, Lee Scanlon, Anthony Schroeder, Mary S. Strine, and David J. Vergobbi have all contributed to this text.

Colleagues from Northern Arizona University, Marist College, and Eastern Connecticut State University all contribute to the pedagogy of the manuscript. I would like to thank Norm Medoff, Dale Hoskins, Brian Snow, Paul Neuman, and Phil Stewart from NAU. Jaime Gomez, Denise Matthews, Paul Melmer, and Nick Messina deserve a great deal of credit for tolerating my presence in the ECSU studio.

I would like to thank all of my former students, near and far, and especially Robby Messer at KTVX, ABC-Channel 4 in Salt Lake City, Utah and Kacie Warner at ESPN in Bristol, Connecticut.

Becky Golden-Harrell, Elinor Actipis, and Robin Weston are my patient and tolerant guides at Focal Press.

Manuscript review was patiently handled by Chris Pruszynski at SUNY Geneseo, David Liban at the University of Colorado at Denver, and Mark Kershaw in the United Kingdom.

I would like to thank Ann Tran at ARRI, Ellen Ryan at Chryon, Kelly Dunworth for Grass Valley, Roger Pujol at Altman Lighting, Megan Bruce and Murray Porteous at Telex, Doug Kanczuzewski at HighTech Furnishings, Kyle Ritland at Mackie, Doug Erickson at Tektronix, Joanne Camarda at Listec Video, Lynne Sauve at Ultimatte, Paul Neuman, Monica O'Connor, and Martin Seymour for assisting with the image package.

I owe the initial momentum of the project to Norman Medoff at Northern Arizona University.

Overview of Equipment and Positions:
The Studio and the Control Room

Introduction

Studio-based television production is not rocket science. To understand the process of studio production is to a large extent a task of learning a new vocabulary, and to a lesser extent a task of learning how to operate the machines of television production.

Technical proficiency is gained in any television production environment through practice, rehearsal, and repetition. The only path to true fluency in any crew position is the practical performance of studio television work in a professional environment. And, although a great deal of knowledge awaits the television student "on the job," much can be mastered prior to that first production position or internship.

The content that is provided here is limited to the most common jobs associated with the studio and the control room. Depending on the size of the television operation, the number of production personnel and their specific job duties will vary widely. For example, in small market stations, the Director not only calls or "cues" the show, but also operates the video switcher and may be responsible for timing video clips as well.

A great deal of geographic (and program genre) variation exists in any given studio production protocol. The "way it is done" in New York will likely differ from the "way it is done" in Des Moines. What follows is a lowest common denominator approach—it is not and does not claim to be exhaustive. International variations (when known) are indicated in text and will be included in the glossary.

The running example in the book is the affiliate-level live television newscast. Not only is the newscast a common form of studio production, it is also a complex one. It is hoped that mastering a news protocol will permit the student of television production to work within other genres with relative ease. Almost all of what follows applies to any studio-based television program—live or taped.

The section that follows provides an overview of the jobs associated with studio-based television production. In addition, for each crew position, the equipment related to each job will be described.

The Television Production Environment

The production environment for the typical network affiliate newscast can be best understood by dividing the television workspace as follows: the studio, the control room, post-production, and Master Control.

The studio and the control room

The **studio** is the large space where the set for a television program is located. For a news program, the anchors deliver the newscast live from an anchor desk to the viewers. Although it is unusual, some studios contain more than one set (for different programs). Commonly, the studio will contain smaller subsets that are used in conjunction with the newscast.

The **control room** is usually nearby. Often the control room is attached to the studio by a common wall (with or without windows). However, it is not uncommon for the control room to be located some distance away from the studio (even on a separate floor of a large building). The control room controls the operations of the studio. While control rooms are usually dedicated to a particular studio, it is important to note that some control rooms can control more than one studio.

Post-production and Master Control

Post-production refers to a space in the television station where editing activities are conducted. In some stations, editing suites (small rooms) are available and contain the equipment necessary for creating any pre-recorded material that can be used in the newscast. As many stations move to server-based, nonlinear systems or portable editing systems, editing can occur just about anywhere at the station or in the field.

Master Control refers to the transmission control of the television station itself. Incoming and outgoing microwave and satellite signals are received/transmitted in this area and the final output mix of the station is controlled here.

Television Control Room

The Studio

The physical space

The studio is designed to control light and sound. The physical space is constructed toward this purpose—to some degree—and all studios will share some of the following characteristics. The studio floor is flat and clean so that the cameras can move smoothly around the set. The production staff needs to help keep the floor clean by avoiding practices that create hazards for the cameras (like spiking the floor with tape).

The walls of the studio can be constructed of many types of material (cinderblock, brick, concrete, etc.). If the walls of your studio are stretched fabric, you need to take special care not to touch, puncture, or tear the fabric membrane as it is designed to absorb sound.

A few feet out from the physical wall, large curtains of fabric called **cycloramas** are common in television studios. Cycloramas, sometimes called "cycs," come in many colors, and most studios will have two or more that surround all or most of the studio. The ceiling of the studio is high in order to accommodate set materials and the studio lighting system. The studio ceiling may be painted black in order to prevent light reflection.

The most prominent feature near the ceiling is the **lighting grid**. The lighting grid is made up of pipes called **battens** (or barrels), and the **lighting instruments** hang from these with large c-clamp mounts. Another item that will be located either in the studio or in the control room is the **lighting board,** which is a computerized "on/off switch" for each lighting instrument. Each instrument can be addressed independently or "tied" to other instruments, and all of the instruments can be controlled at once using the lighting board. The crew members who are responsible for hanging and aiming the lights are called **Gaffers.**

Studio television cameras

The typical studio will be equipped with three studio television cameras. Although many studios have more than three cameras, it would be unusual to find fewer in a typical setup. Studio television cameras are non–format-specific. In other words, the video signal that is generated (analog or digital) can be recorded onto almost any video format. (A camcorder, on the other hand, is a format-specific device.)

All modern studios will be equipped with (at least) standard-definition digital cameras (SDTV), and a few have high-definition cameras (HDTV). The cameras will be numbered Camera One, Two, and Three. The production personnel who operate the cameras are called Camera Operators, and they will be referred to by number. For instance, you might hear, "Hey Camera Two, would you help me move the cyc?" A growing number of studios have robotic cameras that can be controlled by joystick and a computer program. In the case of robotic cameras, only one production crew member is needed to "drive" them.

Television Studio

(Courtesy of Paul Neuman.)

Lighting Grid

The Studio II

The news set

The set for the typical television news program is often centered around a desk where the anchors sit to deliver the program content. The desk is designed to accommodate four anchors at a time (two news anchors, sports, and weather), although all four are rarely seated at the same time.

In most studios, the desk is part of a permanent set that may include **risers** (platforms to raise the height of the desk) and **flats** (vertical panels that provide a background). Numerous **video monitors** (industrial strength television sets) will be positioned throughout the studio as well. The production crew member responsible for assembling the set is called a **Grip** (or Dolly Operator).

Since most news operations use a permanent news set, Grips are not needed on a frequent basis. Commonly, stations will contract set-design firms to design, build, and install the news set.

The weather forecast is delivered from a spot in front of a green screen or chroma key-colored cyclorama (or **chroma key wall**) near the set. The unusual color of the background permits the weather anchor's camera to be keyed over (or layered over) the weather graphics. In this manner, the weather anchor appears to "float" in the foreground, over the graphics.

Patch panels and signal routing

Located on the wall of the studio—often in many locations—are hookup jacks for audio, video, clock, intercom, and other signals that pass between the studio and the control room. These hookup jacks are located together in what is called a **patch panel**.

Prior to the show, the person responsible for audio in the control room will connect cables to route the audio signals from the microphones to a patch panel (and thus into the control room). In some studios, the audio is routed to the patch panel through an **audio snake** that permits multiple mic hookups.

Other members of the production crew may need to make connections to the patch panels as well. Program video may need to be routed to monitors, intercom connections may need to be made, and even cameras can (in some studios) be hooked into different panels. It is not uncommon to find a **routing switcher** inside of the studio as well. Routing switchers permit audio and video signals to be "sent" to different (and sometimes multiple) locations in the studio and control room.

A Simple News Desk with Flats

(Courtesy of Martin Seymour.)

The Studio III

Floor Director
The boss of the studio is called the **Floor Director** (or Floor Manager). The Floor Director's primary job is to communicate with, or cue, the news anchors. The Floor Director can hear the commands of the Director using an intercom system that links the studio to the control room. The Floor Director will cue using voice commands or by using hand signals when a microphone is active, so it is important to not only listen to but also to watch the Floor Director.

In addition to cueing the anchors, the Floor Director communicates with the entire studio staff. In the ideal situation, the Floor Director has some experience with operating cameras, lighting, set assembly, and audio procedures. He or she is frequently called upon to assist the other studio personnel and to help troubleshoot equipment problems. Often, the Floor Director is responsible for studio safety as well. As the Director's eyes, ears, and mouth in the studio, the Floor Director is the ultimate authority in the studio once the program begins. In this way, the Floor Director acts as the Director's representative in the studio.

The Floor Director also acts as a host in the studio for the news anchors and any guests that may be included in the program. Floor Directors help anchors and guests put on microphones and "dress" the mic cables. While the Floor Director can "talk back" to the Director, it is poor form for any of the production staff to use the intercom system to chat.

Talent
Finally, the talent of the news program, the anchors (or presenters), work in the studio during the live portion of the program. Typically, about 10 minutes before the program begins, the anchors will be seated on the set, and mic checks will be conducted (along with other technical checks). Often, the anchors will spend the last few minutes before the show goes live reviewing and editing a hard (or paper) copy of the script.

The Floor Director will review any unusual events for the program with the anchors and the rest of the studio crew as necessary (guest interviews, special camera moves, etc.). In most network affiliate newscasts, the talent consists of two news anchors (one who is often "senior" in status), a weather anchor, and a sports anchor.

A Floor Director Showing Cue to Stand By

(Courtesy of Martin Seymour.)

The Control Room

Equipment and crew positions

The control room "controls" the studio. While a wide array of audio and video processing gear will be installed in the control room, and all control rooms will differ to some extent, most will include the following: a **monitor wall**, an **audio console**, a **video switcher**, a **teleprompting computer**, a **graphics computer**, an **engineering** space, and a section for **VTR** (video tape recorder) control.

Monitor wall

The monitor wall is centered around two larger video monitors that display **preview** video and **program** video. The program video monitor displays the video source that is active, live, online, or the video signal that is being recorded or viewed at home. The preview monitor shows the video source that is next or "on deck" for a program.

Surrounding these two large monitors are smaller video monitors that display the video sources available for use by the production crew. These smaller monitors will show studio cameras, microwave feeds, satellite feeds, graphics, and other video sources that can be activated or routed to "preview" and "program."

The video switcher and Technical Director

A prominent feature of the control room is the **video switcher** (or vision mixer), which is a video selection device. The switcher controls the video sources that are activated to preview and program and is operated by the **Technical Director (TD)** (or Vision Mixer, VM). The final video feed from the video switcher is called **Video Program**. The video switcher is discussed in detail in the following chapter as is another prominent feature of the control room: the **audio board.**

The audio board and Audio Operator

The audio board may be located in the control room proper (with everything else), or it is not uncommon to find it in a smaller adjacent room (audio booth). The audio board is an audio selection device that is operated by a crew member called the **Audio Operator**, or just **"Audio."** The audio feed from the audio board (the final mix) is called **Audio Program. Audio monitors**—heavy-duty speakers—will be located near the monitor wall to permit the control room crew to listen to the program.

Video Switcher

(Courtesy of Grass Valley.)

Audio Board

(Courtesy of Mackie.)

13

Production Crew

The graphics computer and "Graphics"
The graphics computer is operated by a crew member who is commonly called "**Graphics.**" The **graphics computer** can create, store, and recall two kinds of graphics: **character generation (CG)** (or caption generator) and **electronic still-store (ESS).** CG is the creation of alphanumeric text as a video signal. A good example of CG is when the anchor's name is keyed (or layered) over a camera shot or at the end of the program when the credits are "rolled."
   The ESS function centers around still-image processing. The graphics computer can store high-resolution images, capture images from other video sources, and combine these images with CG to create entirely new graphics. A good example of ESS is when a still image of a reporter is displayed during a phoned-in report or a report without video. It is important to note that many control rooms will divide the CG and ESS functions into two separate computers, workspaces, and crew positions.

The prompting computer and the "Prompter"
Another computer in the control room is the **prompting computer.** The prompting computer transforms the script for the show into a scrollable video signal that is transmitted to a viewing system on the front of the studio cameras.
   The **Prompter** position controls the word processing and organization of the final script for the program. The collation of all of the stories occurs in the prompting computer, and all final changes to the script are made by the producing staff through this computer system. The person who operates the prompting computer is called the "**Prompter.**"

Video tape recorders and "Tape"
The television program is recorded and any pre-recorded material needed for the show is controlled from the "**Tape**" position. Tape is responsible for operating numerous **video tape recorders** (VTRs) or other video playback devices (computer-based). Pre-recorded material is then "rolled" from tape (or a video server), as needed and in order. A good example of this is when a sports anchor is discussing a basketball game from earlier in the day and the viewer is watching the taped or pre-recorded footage of that game.
   It is important to note that in many control rooms, the VTR racks (and therefore the Tape Operator) are located in an adjacent room (as is common with audio). The number of VTRs available will vary by facility. For a typical newscast, at least four VTRs will be utilized (one to record, three for playback) for greatest efficiency. Be aware that a common tactic is to "letter" VTRs (VTR A, VTR B, etc.), in order to avoid confusion with the "numbered" cameras (Camera One, Camera Two, etc.).

Video Tape Recorder Rack

(Courtesy of High Tech Furnishings.)

15

Production Crew II

The Broadcast Engineer

The task of the **Broadcast Engineer** during a live production is twofold. First, all audio and video signal routing is this person's responsibility. Live feeds, for example, will need to be routed as sources to the control room on an as-needed basis. Another example is the appropriate routing of video and audio signals both to and from the VTRs.

Second, the Broadcast Engineer performs any equipment troubleshooting during routing procedures. Prior to and during the show, the Engineer is responsible for the **camera control units (CCUs),** remote controls for the studio cameras. Before the show, the Engineer must white-balance and register the cameras. By using the waveform monitor and vectorscope, the Engineer can adjust how each camera "sees" individual colors (like red, green, blue, black, and white) so that the cameras are "balanced" or matched. During the program, the Engineer can use the CCUs to make adjustments to the iris settings on the camera lens or to "ride gain" — adjust the strength of the video signal level as needed.

Assistant Director (AD)

Live television programs have to begin and end on time. The responsibility of timing a show (both forward and backward) belongs to the **Assistant Director (AD)** (or Production Assistant). The AD will use a master clock in order to accomplish show timing. The clock will either be set to count up from zero or count down from a preset show length (like 28:30). In this manner, the AD can announce information such as "we are 10 minutes into the show and we have 18 minutes 30 seconds left."

Another very important job for the AD is the timing of any pre-recorded material used for the show. The AD will need to know the precise length of each video clip to be used in the program. This way, the AD knows exactly when the clip will end (so a smooth transition can be made back to the studio) and when graphics can be used in conjunction with the tape. In order to accomplish clip timing, an AD will use a stopwatch. Often, the stopwatch of choice for Assistant Directors is an old-fashioned analog watch (like the *60 Minutes* watch) rather than the more common digital stopwatch (more on this in the Assistant Directing and Directing chapter). It is important to remember that the Assistant Director's job is to handle timing, not merely to "assist" the Director as a gopher.

If a station does not use an AD, it is common for the Producer of the newscast to handle timing the show and for the Director to take charge of clip and graphics timing.

Waveform and Vectorscope

(Courtesy of Tektronix.)

Directing and Producing

Director

Finally, the Director is the leader and supervisor of the entire production crew. During the actual program, the Director "cues" or "calls" commands to the production crew using the intercom system. While the Director usually does not operate any particular piece of equipment, he or she does use the script to call audio and video transitions for the duration of the program.

The most effective directors are very familiar with all of the crew positions and responsibilities as well as much of the production equipment. New directors find that it is very difficult to lead and supervise that which they do not understand. During the program, when the studio is "live," the Director is at the top of the personnel hierarchy. However, a television newscast is a co-creation between the Producer and the Director.

Producer

The **Producer** is the person responsible for the content of the program—the scripts, the stories, and the tapes included. Prior to the broadcast, the Producer works with news, weather, and sports personnel to plan and construct the newscast. The Producer is at the top of the hierarchy before the program begins and after the program ends. This is not to say that the relationship between the Producer and the Director must be adversarial or a power struggle. It is simply that, as a production crew member, it is important to know whom to listen to and when.

The Producer will be located in the control room during the show. He or she may make content changes on the fly that the production crew will need to respond to (like adding or cutting a story). The Producer may also need to communicate with the anchors during the show using the **interrupt foldback (IFB)** system (the little earpiece in the anchor's ear is a speaker that permits the Producer to "cut into" Audio Program in order to speak to the anchor).

Control Room in Action

(Courtesy of High Tech Furnishings.)

Audio Control and Technical Directing

Introduction

The production tasks associated with audio and video control in the production environment are the primary responsibility of two important production technicians: the **Audio Operator** and the **Technical Director (TD)**. The tasks associated with these positions are detailed in this chapter. Both jobs are located in control spaces apart from the studio.

Usually, the audio control space will be located either in the control room itself or in an isolated booth nearby. The booth style of audio facility permits the technician to concentrate on the characteristics of the program audio with greater clarity, apart from the distractions of the rest of the control space. The primary job of Audio is to control Audio Program, which is the final mix of audio that is sent out for transmission or recorded.

The primary job of the Technical Director is to operate the video switcher according to the Director's commands—thus controlling Video Program. The TD is located in the control room, usually near the Director, and at the video switcher. Video Program, much like Audio Program, is the final compilation of video sources that is sent out for transmission or recorded.

Audio Control

The primary responsibility of the technician in charge of audio in a studio production environment is to operate the audio board or "console." The job is often simply called "Audio," rather than "Audio Operator" or some other title. Audio anticipates and responds to commands from the Director, activating and mixing audio sources to Audio Program as needed and on demand. To understand the job of Audio, one must first understand the basics of audio board operation.

The audio board

An audio board is an audio selection device. Common audio sources that Audio can select from include the studio microphones: MIC 1, MIC 2, and MIC 3; audio from the video tape recorders: VTR A track 1 or Left Channel, VTR A track 2 or Right Channel, VTR B track 1, VTR B track 2; an audio or video file server of some kind; a satellite feed: SAT; a microwave feed: sometimes indicated as MX; and CD players: CD1 L, CD1 R, CD2 L, CD2 R. In addition, the audio board itself is an audio source, providing test tones, for example. (It is important to remember that one could have any number of microphones, VTRs, satellite and microwave feeds, as well as other sources, depending on the facility.)

The lake of audio

In order to better understand how an audio board works, consider the following conceptual description: for now, go with the idea that the audio board is like a large lake—a lake of audio. Flowing into the lake are many individual streams of audio, and each stream represents a source of audio (like a microphone). Flowing out of the lake is one river of audio: **Audio Program**—the final mix that is recorded or heard through the speakers of the television set at home.

The Lake of Audio

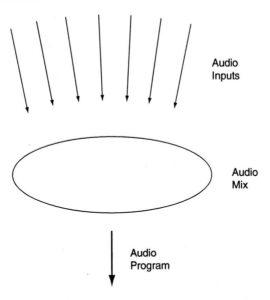

Audio
Inputs

Audio
Mix

Audio
Program

Audio Flow

Input and output faders

A typical audio board will have a group of **faders** (knobs that slide up and down) along the bottom of the panel, located closest to the operator. Most of the faders control audio sources or inputs—these begin on the absolute left of the board, continue across the middle of the console, and end (usually) at about three-quarters of the way across.

The faders located from this point onward—the right-hand quarter of the console—control the output of the board. Usually, a fader with a red knob indicates the **master fader,** which ultimately controls the strength of Audio Program—normally this fader is the last one on the right side of the board. The other faders in the right quarter are submaster outputs or auxiliary "send" controls.

Audio sources will either be **mono** or **stereo.** For example, microphones are mono sources and CD players are stereo sources. Mono means that the source is generating one unique, individual, and distinct channel or "line" of audio. Stereo means that the source is generating or has the capacity to generate two unique, individual, and distinct channels or lines of audio.

VTRs, generally speaking, can generate two channels of source audio and are handled as stereo sources—even if in a given instance only one channel of a tape contains audio. The important idea to retain here is that some sources will be controlled with one fader and others with two.

The audio flow

Again, consider the lake of audio example. Each input fader (or source) is like a dam that controls the flow of audio into the lake. When the fader is "up," the audio is flowing. When the fader is down, the audio flow is stopped. Each output fader—and you should focus on the master fader at this point—also controls audio flow like a dam. When the master fader is up, the audio may flow out of the lake. When the master fader is down, the audio is held within the lake.

It is possible, then, to (1) allow audio to flow in and out—through the lake (both an input fader and the master fader are pushed up); (2) to allow audio to flow in and not out (an input fader is pushed up and the master fader is pushed down); or (3) to allow no flow at all (all faders down). The volume of audio that flows into, through, and out of the lake is thus determined by the position of each little "dam" (fader) in the audio stream. You can see, then, how it is possible that two sources can flow into the lake individually, be combined together, and then flow out in the final river of Audio Program (or the "mix"). The flow of audio is measured in terms of signal strength, which is covered in the next section.

Input Fader

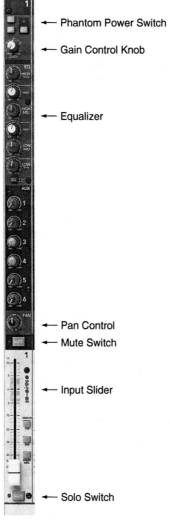

← Phantom Power Switch

← Gain Control Knob

← Equalizer

← Pan Control

← Mute Switch

← Input Slider

← Solo Switch

(Courtesy of Mackie.)

27

Signal Strength

Volume and **signal strength** are two separate concepts from the same family. Volume is a human perception of loudness. Signal strength, on the other hand, is a measurement of how much voltage is associated with an audio signal. The primary concern for the crew member assigned to the Audio position is how strong an audio signal is, not how loud it seems.

In order to adjust the strength of an audio signal, the input stream and the output stream (Audio Program) must be measured. The two common analog measurements for audio are the **volume unit (VU)** and the **percentage of modulation (PM)**. Using these measures, a signal flow is ideal at an average peak of 0VU or 100PM. However, as digital audio processing becomes more the norm, Audio Technicians will need to shift measures to the **decibel** scale **(dB)**. A digital signal flow is ideal at an average peak of –20dB.

The primary task for Audio is to monitor and adjust signal flow during the program using each input fader and the master output fader. Signal flow above the ideal risks **overmodulation,** noise, and distortion. Signal flow below the ideal is weak, perhaps imperceptible—this is called "**undermodulation.**" The only way to monitor signal flow is by using the meters located on the audio board itself.

Audio operations

One of the more common issues associated with operating an audio board is when an audio source is flowing either too high or too low. To adjust a high flowing source, the usual fix is to merely push the input fader down for that source—thus limiting the incoming flow. As long as the source is not distorting at capture (like a politician screaming into a mic), the signal should be easily attenuated by fading down.

Adjusting a low flowing source, however, is a bit more difficult—one can only "open the dam" so far. And audio sources differ in terms of their relative origin strength, as well. **Line sources,** like CD players, have relatively strong signals from the get-go. The signal from a microphone (a **mic source**), on the other hand, can be as much as 50dB weaker than a line source.

In order to balance all of this out, most consoles will have an area near the top of the fader strip labeled **"trim"** or **"gain."** By adjusting the Gain knob, the incoming signal or flow of an audio source can be made stronger or reduced as needed. If faced with a low flowing audio source, one would fade up as high as possible on the source fader and then turn to the gain control for amplification of the incoming audio signal. Be aware, however, that a risk of using the gain to amplify low audio levels is that noise in the audio signal will be amplified as well.

Top of Input Fader Showing Gain Control and Equalizer

Audio Board Fader Strip Top Third

◄——— Phantom Power Switch

◄——— Gain Control Knob

◄——— Equalizer

(Courtesy of Mackie.)

Signal Processing

Audio consoles will usually permit some signal processing of the audio sources beyond the raw manipulation of signal strength. Simple **equalization** tasks are usually handled in the fader strip with knobs dedicated to low, middle, and high ranges. **Filtering**, if available on your console, will also be located on the fader strip. An equalizer merely boosts or reduces signal strength within a given set of frequencies. A filter, on the other hand, marks a frequency and then reduces all signals below or above the mark.

Depending on the manufacturer of your console, other controls may be located on the fader strip. **Solo** allows you to isolate and listen to a given source for monitoring purposes without affecting the overall mix of Audio Program. Solo is useful, for example, in adjusting a troublesome source while in the middle of a live program. **Pan** is another common control. Pan allows you to "send" a given source left or right in the overall output mix. Using Pan, one could "send," if you will, a mic source only to the right speaker.

Phantom power is a feature built into many audio consoles. Phantom power—48 volts of direct current (DC)—sends power back down the input line (on the grounding wire) and is used to power capacitor microphones without the need for a battery.

In addition to the input fader strips and master fader, the audio console will likely contain controls that adjust monitor volume in the control room and (if so equipped) in the studio. Monitor volume will need to be adjusted in the control room largely to the level preferred by the Director. In the typical newscast, studio monitors would be in the "off" position, as they are not needed.

The major audio feed that is required to be patched back into the studio is known as **IFB** (**interrupt foldback** or interrupt feedback). The plastic "bug" that you can see hooked into the ear of the anchor allows him or her to monitor Audio Program during the show. The anchors can hear the entire program mix (excluding the anchor's own microphone—called "mix minus") and can therefore monitor any pre-recorded material as it is played back in the show. The important part of IFB is the "interrupt" feature. The IFB allows anyone in the control room (usually a producer) to speak directly to the anchor through the audio console. In doing so, a producer could alert the anchor to a breaking news item or to some other change in the show. IFB is also called "switched talkback."

Studio audio
The task of hooking up and connecting microphones in the studio is often shared with the Floor Director. For a description, see the "Microphones and Sound Check" section on page 94.

IFB Earset

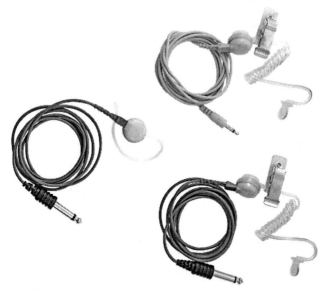

(Courtesy of Telex.)

IFB Beltpack

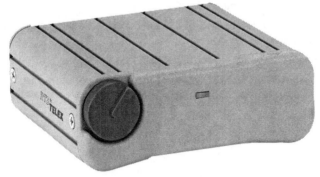

(Courtesy of Telex.)

31

Audio and the Director

The directing commands that Audio must respond to are numerous. However, a good director will always give Audio a "ready" cue and a "do it" cue of some kind. The left hand of Audio covers the input faders and the right hand covers the master fader area. Consider the following examples:

Example One:

Director says, "Ready Camera One with her mic and a cue."

Audio identifies input fader of relevant microphone.

Director says, "Take Camera One, mic, and cue."

Audio pushes fader up to zero mark and then adjusts fader position based on meter indication.

Example Two:

Director says, "Stand by Tape A, full track is coming on A."

Audio identifies the two input faders of VTR A.

Director says, "Roll Tape A, track, and take."

Audio pushes both faders up to zero mark and then adjusts fader position based on meter indication.

Example Three:

Director says, "Ready music from your CD."

Audio identifies input faders of CD player and cues CD track (by putting player on "pause").

Director says, "**Go** music (or go sound)."

Audio pushes "Play" on CD player (or releases pause) and pushes both faders up to zero mark and then adjusts fader position based on meter indication.

Audio Control Booth

(Courtesy of Telex.)

Technical Director/Video Switcher

As mentioned earlier in this chapter, the primary responsibility of the Technical Director (TD) (or Vision Mixer) in a studio production environment is to operate the video switcher (or vision mixer). The TD anticipates and responds to commands from the Director, activating video sources to Video Program as needed and on demand. To understand the job of the TD, one must first understand the basics of switcher operation.

The video switcher

A video switcher is a video selection device. Common video sources that the TD can select from include the studio cameras: Camera One, Camera Two, and Camera Three; the video tape recorders: VTR A, VTR B, and VTR C; a video file server of some kind: sometimes indicated as HD; a satellite feed: SAT; a microwave feed: sometimes indicated as MX; graphics computers: CG or ESS or motion graphics/3D; and the switcher itself: color bars, color backgrounds, including black. (It is important to remember that one could have any number of cameras, VTRs, satellite and microwave feeds, and graphics computers, depending on the facility.)

The mix effects bus (M/E)

A typical video switcher will have a group of three rows of buttons located in the lower left area of the console (some only have two rows, and a few have four rows). Many switchers will have more than one group of three rows of buttons, and each group of three rows is called a mix effects bus or M/E. If your switcher has more than one M/E, they will be numbered (M/E 1, M/E 2).

For now, focus upon the M/E that is closest to the front of the console and nearest to the TD. The bottom row of buttons is called the **preview bus,** the middle row is called the **program bus,** and the top row (if your switcher is so equipped) is called the **key bus.** Note that each of the three rows of buttons is identical—for example, in the bottom row, the first button might be labeled "Black." If this is the case, the first button of the second row and the first button of the third row will also be labeled "Black." Each button represents a video source and, when pressed, selects or activates that particular source in the selected bus.

The preview bus

When you press "Camera One" in the preview bus, the video signal being generated by Camera One appears in the preview monitor. If you press "Bars" in the preview bus, color bars appear in the preview monitor. Remember, preview is the video signal that is "on deck" or next.

When the Director wants to activate a signal to "preview," he or she will call a ready cue or a stand-by cue. For example, "Ready Camera One" is a command for the TD to activate Camera One in the preview bus. "Stand by Tape A" is a command for the TD to activate VTR A in the preview bus. Savvy directors will use the term "ready" for cameras and the term "stand by" for tapes to facilitate communication with the production crew.

Video Switcher

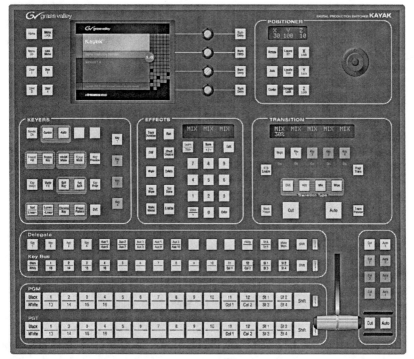

(Courtesy of Grass Valley.)

The Program Bus and the Key Bus

The program bus

When you press "Camera One" in the program bus, the video signal being generated by Camera One appears in the program monitor. Remember that Video Program is the video signal that is "hot" or "live"—it is what everyone at home is watching (when the studio is live) or the signal that is being recorded.

Therefore, it is important to be very careful with the buttons in the program bus when the facility is in production—if you press a button in the program bus, the associated video source goes directly to program. In pre-production or post-production situations (before the show or after the show), the TD will often select directly from the program bus for efficiency. At these points, there is little worry of accidentally selecting the "wrong" video source. The video source selected in the program bus is also called the "video background."

The key bus

If your switcher is equipped with a third row of buttons in the M/E (or a fourth), the row is called the key bus. The video source that is selected here will be activated as a key source. To understand the key bus, one must understand what a key is. A key is merely a "video layer" that is independently selected and controlled from the "video background."

The video background is the video source selected in the program bus (see above). The key source is the video source associated with the button selected in the key bus. Any video source can be a key and any can be the background. Therefore, any video source can be "keyed over" any other. Commonly, a graphics computer of some kind (usually functioning in character generator mode) is selected as a key source.

Once selected, written material can then be keyed over the background video (usually a camera or tape). For example, when an anchor's name pops up on the screen over his or her image, the key has been activated and the key source is some kind of graphics computer in CG mode or a separate CG source.

Keys get confusing. Depending on the switcher, one can activate multiple keys in multiple M/E buses. It is possible, then, to be viewing multiple video sources at the same time in the program monitor. (A good example of this is CNN's *Headline News* programming.)

Routing a video source through a DVE (a special effects generator) can make the keying process even more confusing. For example, if the graphics computer is displaying an ESS (a still picture) of a fire, the ESS is assigned to the DVE, the DVE is creating a quarter-screen box, and the DVE is keyed over a camera, one gets a "box" effect. For now, remember that a key is a separate video source that is independently controlled from the preview and program busses.

Preview Bus, Program Bus, Key Bus

(Courtesy of Grass Valley.)

Flip-Flop Switching

In order to select a video source to preview or to program, the TD merely presses the button that corresponds to the video source desired. To actually switch a live show, however, the TD will "flip-flop" switch—in other words, the TD will activate a source to preview and then transition that source (or move that source) to program in one of three ways: **cut, wipe,** or **dissolve.**

On most switchers, the transition control area is immediately to the right of the M/E bus (see figure on page 39). The usual setup includes a button that is labeled "Cut" next to a button labeled "Auto" or "Auto Trans." Immediately adjacent to or above the "Cut" and "Auto Trans" buttons are two more buttons: "Wipe" and "Mix." If so equipped, a switcher may also have a fader bar located in the transition area as well.

Above the "Wipe" and "Mix" buttons will be at least one button labeled BKGD for "Background" and at least one KEY button. The BKGD button is normally active all the time. The KEY button is normally not active. Essentially, by depressing one or the other or both, you are telling the switcher what video (the background, the key, or both) to address in the following transitions.

The cut

The process to "cut" a source from preview to program is simple. The TD will make sure the BKGD button is active and the KEY button is not. The TD will select the source desired in the preview bus and press the "Cut" button in the transition area. The selected source will transition (instantly) from preview to program.

For example, consider the following commands from a Director: "Ready Camera One," and "Take Camera One." At the "ready" cue, the TD will press the Camera One button in the preview bus. At the "Take" command, the TD will press the Cut button in the transition area. ("Take" is the directing command for the TD to activate a "Cut" transition.)

The dissolve

The process to dissolve to a source selected in the preview bus is similar. The TD will make sure the BKGD button is active and the KEY button is not. The TD will activate the "Mix" button (this will deactivate the "Wipe" button and set up the switcher so that the next transition effect will be a dissolve). The TD will select the source desired in the preview bus. At this point, the TD will either punch the "Auto Trans" button (engaging an automatic dissolve) or manually grasp the fader bar to pull (or push) the dissolve.

For example, consider the following commands from a Director: "Ready Camera One, we will dissolve," and "Dissolve." At the "ready" cue, the TD will press the Camera One button in the preview bus and prepare for a dissolve. At the "Dissolve" command, the TD (in this case) will punch the "Auto Trans" button.

Switcher Transition Area

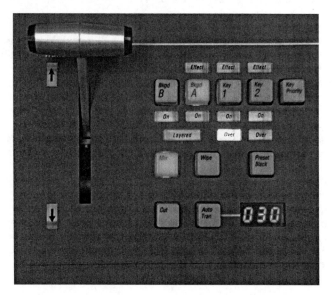

Additional Transitions

The fader bar

If the Director says, "Ready Camera One, we will dissolve, and I want you to pull (or push) it," the TD merely uses the fader bar instead of the "Auto Trans" button to engage the dissolve effect.

A note is warranted about production terminology at this point. The command to "Fade" is often used interchangeably with the command "Dissolve." A fade indicates that the transition is to utilize the "black" video source in a dissolve effect. The TD, then, can "fade to black" or "fade up from black" but cannot fade from Camera One to Camera Two. However, usage is particular to the Director at hand and, ultimately, will vary.

The wipe

The final transition is the wipe. Wipes are engaged in almost the exact same manner as dissolves but carry an important extra step in the process. To engage a wipe effect to the video source selected in preview, the TD will make sure the BKGD button is active and the KEY button is not. The TD will activate the "Wipe" button (this will deactivate the "Mix" button and set up the switcher so that the next transition effect will be a wipe). The TD will now select a wipe pattern—the extra step.

Wipe patterns

Wipe patterns determine the geometric shape of the wipe. Depending on the video switcher, numerous wipe patterns are available to select from— circles, squares, triangles, rectangles, stars, clock arms (the Batman effect), straight line (top, bottom, left, and right), and digital patterns are a few of the common ones.

Once a pattern is selected, multiple characteristics of the wipe pattern can be manipulated, depending on the switcher capability—border, edge softness or hardness (blur), border thickness, border color, pattern position, rotation, rotation speed, pattern duplicates (i.e., two or more stars), aspect ratio, and so forth.

Once the wipe pattern and its characteristics are set, the TD will either punch the "Auto Trans" button (engaging an automatic wipe) or manually grasp the fader bar to pull (or push) the wipe.

For example, consider the following commands from a Director: "Ready Camera One, we will wipe," and "Wipe." At the "ready" cue, the TD will press the Camera One button in the preview bus and prepare for the wipe. At the "Wipe" command, the TD (in this case) will punch the "Auto Trans" button. If the Director says, "Ready Camera One, we will wipe, and I want you to pull (or push) it," the TD merely uses the fader bar instead of the "Auto Trans" button to engage the wipe effect.

Switcher Wipe Pattern-Select Area

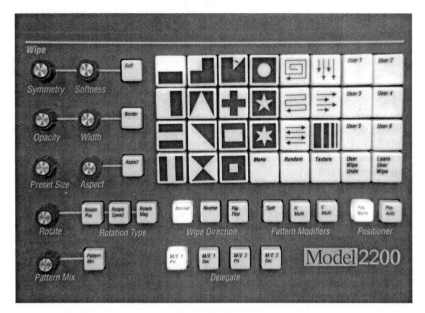

A Key Is a Video Layer

Keying
In order to select a key source, the TD will depress the appropriate button of the desired video source in the key bus. For this discussion, imagine that Camera One is in program, Camera Two is in preview, and the TD has selected the graphics computer as the key source. Furthermore, assume that the name "Roger Hicks" has been typed into the graphics computer and that the name is centered on the computer screen on the bottom line. At this point, the TD has to decide how to activate the key—how to "bring the key on" over the active program source. Even using a basic switcher, the TD has two choices: the midstream key or the downstream key.

The midstream key
The midstream key button (KEY) is located in the transition area next to the background (BKGD) button. To activate the key, the TD will need to activate the KEY button and (in this case) deactivate the BKGD button. The switcher is set up, then, to bring on a key layer (graphics computer) without affecting the existing BKGD (Camera One).

At this point, the TD can "cut" the key on using the "Cut" button, "dissolve" the key on, or "wipe" the key on. If the key is to be dissolved on or wiped on, the TD will need to select the effect desired (mix or wipe) in the transition area and either punch the "Auto Trans" button or engage the fader bar. To remove the key layer, the TD merely cuts, wipes, or dissolves the key source "off."

If the TD desires to transition the background video source BKGD and the key video source KEY at the same time, the TD merely activates both buttons (a double punch) at the top of the transition area. When the transition is activated (cut, wipe, or dissolve), both video sources will change at the same time. The background will change to the video source in preview; the key will merely activate (or deactivate).

The downstream key
Another common way to activate a key is to bring it on in a downstream keyer (DSK). If the switcher has a button labeled "DSK," the TD can activate (and deactivate) the key layer by pressing this switch (probably a cut but sometimes a dissolve). Often the "DSK" button will be located immediately to the right of the transition area or on the extreme far lower right of the console. It is important to note that the downstream key source, however, is not selected from the key bus, it is usually hardwired.

Similar to the downstream key is a direct key switch. Located in the transition area, a direct keyer will be labeled "KEY 1 Cut" or "KEY 1 Mix" (the layer will either "cut" or "dissolve" on). When activated, the key will appear, layered over the program video source, in much the same manner as a downstream key. Unlike a DSK, a direct key source is selected from the key bus.

Midstream Key Select (Note two separate keys are controlled here: KEY 1 and KEY 2.)

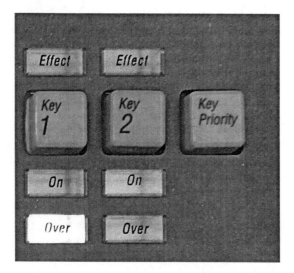

Directing a Key

What video source is where?

Many switchers have more than one midstream key available (KEY 1 and KEY 2). Remember, each is independent of the other and both are controlled in precisely the same manner. The difficult part of the process is keeping track of what video source is assigned to each keyer and which keyer is active—both can be "on" at the same time.

Directing a key

When a Director wants to activate a key, he or she will convey the command to the TD in one of the following ways:

"Stand by Downstream," and "Downstream."
"Stand by Midstream," and Midstream."
"Ready to Font," and "Font."
"Ready to Key," and "Key."

As you can see, there is a great deal of variance in this particular directing command.

Keys can be manipulated in almost as many ways as wipe patterns. Two main key controls are worth mentioning here—**clip** and **gain**. Gain governs the strength of the key source video signal. Clip governs the relative strength of the layer. By adjusting clip and gain, the TD can make sure that the key source is visible but not so strong as to cover over the BKGD source. A good rule of thumb is to crank the gain as high as you can and govern the key layer strength using the clip control.

The Technical Director and the Director

The directing commands that a TD must respond to are numerous. However, a good director will always give the TD a "ready" cue and a "Do It" cue of some kind. The left hand of the TD covers the preview bus (much like a typewriter) and the right hand covers the transition area. Consider the following examples:

Example One:

Director says, "Ready Camera One."

TD selects Camera One in preview.

Director says, "Take Camera One."

TD punches the "Cut" button.

Example Two:

Director says, "Ready to wipe to Camera Three."

TD selects Camera Three in preview, makes sure BKGD is active and KEY is not (default), selects Wipe in the transition area (and has previously selected the pattern and the pattern characteristics if any).

Director says, "Wipe to Camera Three."

TD punches the "Auto Trans" button.

Example Three:

Director says, "Stand by Tape A, full track is coming on A."

TD selects VTR A in preview.

Director says, "Roll Tape A, track, and take."

TD will punch "Cut" button on the take command.

Directing Audio/Directing the TD

In addition to the usual concerns associated with directing a live television program, a few unique issues present themselves concerning Audio and the TD. For both positions, consider that the primary responsibility of the assigned technicians is to anticipate and respond to commands from the Director. The Director must be able to communicate clearly and efficiently to Audio and the TD, without confusion to either.

The Director should always give ready or stand-by cues prior to command cues, and the Director must be consistent with any command language he or she chooses to use. With practice, the technicians will be able to anticipate the Director's needs.

The audiovisual requirements of every newscast will vary. Technical Directors and Audio Technicians will need to be flexible, and to some extent accommodating, in order for the production to be a success. The manner in which live feeds are handled, the procedures for breaking news, and the nuances of the facility will differ from station to station. The most important idea to keep in mind is that success is really defined by the production procedures in place—the more practiced and consistent the production protocols are, the more complicated a show can be. Ideally, any deviance from regular protocols should be well rehearsed prior to transmission.

In many news environments, the separation line between the production folks and the producing staff is not as well defined as it may need to be for the good of the show. Once the show begins, the technicians need to be clear that the boss is the Director, not the Producer or other member of the producing staff. Producers need to be clear on this protocol as well and must refrain from communicating directly to any technician during an actual production.

Lighting and Sets

Introduction

Set design and lighting design are two sides of the same coin. While the traditional mode of set design begins with an assessment of program needs (number of talent, for example), lighting design is a somewhat constricted art due to the specific technical requirements needed to create the video image. Both topics are extensive in their own right and entire courses are based on each. The goal of this chapter is to introduce each in a most basic sense and limited only to the affiliate-level newscast. It is important to note that lighting and set design are tightly limited by the station or program budget, the physical limitations of the studio, and the lighting package available for use in any given setup.

Set Placement

One of the first considerations when undertaking the design process for a studio-installed news set is the physical space of the studio itself. If the studio is to be dedicated to the news program, and no other programs are to utilize the space, the set can pretty much encompass the entire space. If this is the case, the best possible positioning for the news set may be the middle of the studio. The reasoning behind this "centered" placement might not be completely obvious. A centered set increases the number of possible camera angles (360-degree coverage) and greatly increases the possibilities for lighting placement and coverage. Additionally, a centered set creates a great deal of visual depth to nearly every camera composition—an added bonus.

However, most studios will need to accommodate at least one other program, and so the news set will need to "share" the space. The choice will need to be made, then, between parking the set along a wall or moving it into one of the corners. The advantage to using a flat wall stems from maximizing studio space for other program setups. At least three walls in most studios will be usable, and therefore, one could "set" three separate shows along them. In this setup, cameras can "cover" 180 degrees of each set, and the lighting design is still fairly flexible. However, a major disadvantage exists within this construction—visual depth is compromised (and therefore a key ingredient to visual interest—the **Z-Axis**—is lost). In other words, the set appears flat.

A nice compromise between a centered set and a set placed along the wall of the studio is corner placement. When a set is parked in a corner, visual depth is somewhat recreated naturally. Furthermore, at least two other corners of the studio are left for other setups. In a typical news setup, the chroma key area can be naturally joined to the set along an adjacent flat wall space. The disadvantages of corner placement stem from camera angle flexibility (90 degrees) and the generation of some limitation on backlighting placements. If the set is placed in a studio corner, yet well distanced from the cyc, some of these limitations can be minimized.

Overhead View of Corner Set Placements

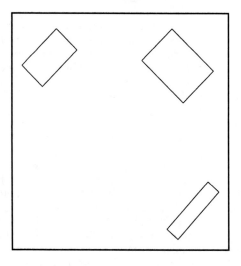

Risers, Flats, Desk

The traditional news set is constructed on an 8- to 10-inch platform made up of **risers**. Risers are merely used to boost the set into the air so that a typical camera angle will remain at eye level to the anchors. Risers permit the Camera Operators to stand normally behind the cameras. Risers will typically be carpeted in order to deaden sound and to enhance appearance. In design terms, risers can also add an element of visual focus to the set.

Placed on top of the risers will be the ubiquitous **news desk**. No part of the set says "news" more clearly than the desk. Perhaps no other set element has been fussed with as much and as frequently as the desk. No matter. Whatever the shape, color, size, or material, the news desk will ideally accommodate up to four anchors at a time (news, news, sports, weather) and must provide a comfortable spot for at least two (the news anchors—as the weather anchor can merely "lean" on the desk).

The sports anchor will sometimes sit along the edge of the desk or may deliver the sports segment from some other dedicated spot in the studio or the sports area of the newsroom. In some colleges and universities, the news desk is not used in order to prevent new reporters from leaning and to encourage good posture. On a few of the national network newscasts, the desk has been abandoned in favor of a standing delivery (and perhaps to encourage good posture).

The background of a news set is often made up of a wall of panels called **flats**. While it is uncommon to find a newscast that does not use a flat wall, some sets permit the viewer to "see through" to the newsroom, or merely permit the background to be a clean view of the studio curtain or cyc. For those news programs that do use a flat wall, the sky is the limit.

In addition, a **duratran** is sometimes used. This is a backlit translucent photograph of cityscapes, landmarks, or local geography that may be embedded in the wall of flats. Video monitors in any number, shape, and combination; columns of light encased in plastic; logos (painted, projected, or video); as well as bookcases, woodwork, maps, glass, chrome, steel, and just about anything else you can think of may become news set backgrounds. The cost of a news set ranges from very little into the millions.

Student Anchors on Set with Floor Director

(Courtesy of Paul Neuman.)

The Weather Wall

Adjacent to the news set will be an area dedicated to delivering the weather forecast. Either a chroma key wall or chroma key-colored cyc will be utilized in order for the weather anchor to appear to "float" in front of the weather graphics. The only real set design consideration for the weather area concerns monitor placement and access to the computer that holds and reads the graphics sequence.

Usually, three monitors will be placed around the chroma key wall in order for the weather anchor to see him or herself in relation to the graphics—one at each end and one to the front. In some fancier setups, the chroma key wall is bound or "framed" by flats or is embedded within the flat wall. Access to the computer that holds the sequence of weather graphics is important in order for the weather anchor to make changes or to intervene in the sequence playback.

Light + set + graphics = look

In nearly all set design considerations for a typical affiliate newscast, a design consultant or broadcast design company will be contracted to design a "look" for the program, and to handle the construction and installation of the set and lighting package. In some cases, a graphics package (logos, colors, fonts, animations) may also be created that are specific to a show, station, or network.

Weather Wall

(Courtesy of Martin Seymour.)

Lighting

At the time a television studio is constructed, an important piece of the overall design and layout will concern the lighting package to be installed. In a permanent set installation, where the studio is dedicated only to the newscast, the lighting package is often customized to (and purchased with) the news set. However, it is also common to find a studio with a general lighting package that can be used for a variety of program needs, and that can be adapted for different uses.

Electrical service (U.S. only)
The lighting package in any given studio begins with the electrical service to the lighting system. Studio lighting requires two to four times the amount of electricity that is required for a stand-alone, single-family home. For example, it is not uncommon to service a typical studio with as much as 600 amps of conditioned power (electricity "fed" through a machine that prevents voltage surges)—with about two-thirds of the service (400 amps) ready for active use.

A more useful guide is to remember that each light that is used in a studio will be serviced with a breaker-protected, individual 20-amp circuit (and is nearly always 120 volts). So, 400 amps of "active" service permits the illumination of 20 lights at any given time, 600 amps would permit the illumination of 30 lights, and so on.

Another point to remember regarding the power service is that a 2,000-watt lamp requires an individual 20-amp circuit. (So, consider that 400 amps of "active" service permits the simultaneous illumination of twenty 20-amp circuits, each using 2,000-watt lamps, for a total illumination of 40,000 watts of lighting power.)

Schematic of a Lighting Grid Used for Lighting and Set Design

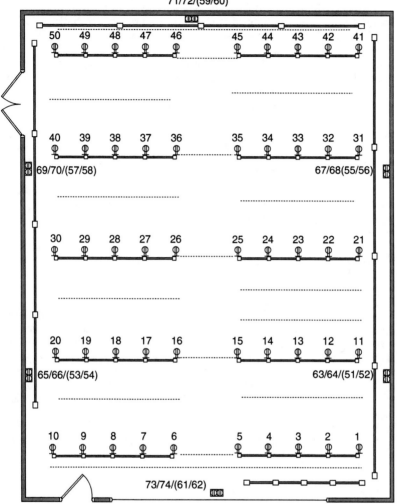

(Courtesy of Paul Melmer.)

The Lighting Grid

The grid of pipes suspended from the ceiling of the studio is called the **lighting grid**. The lighting grid is made up of pipes called **battens** (or **barrels**). In some installations, the lighting grid is fixed; in others, it can be lowered for ease of use.

Each individual light that hangs from the grid is called a **lighting instrument**. Depending on the electrical service to the studio, the grid will be serviced with a number of 20-amp "outlets" that hang from pigtails (short extension cables) connected to the electric system of the studio.

The lighting grid will ideally be located fairly high up off the studio floor to permit as much working headroom as possible for the set installation and to allow for more flexibility with lighting placement. In order to access a fixed grid, the studio will be equipped with nonconductive ladders, a rolling ladder/platform of some fashion, or a scissor lift.

Be aware that lighting tasks are potentially the most dangerous in the studio environment. The risk of injury or death from electrocution or from working well off the ground is very real, and, in the case of a scissor lift system, a moment of distraction can easily result in a severed limb.

Halogen lights become very hot very fast—wear gloves as needed. Never touch a bare halogen light bulb in a studio environment—the oil from your skin will cause the bulb to explode or otherwise fail.

Spot lights and flood lights

The lighting instruments are easily classed into two groups—**spot lights** and **flood lights**. Spot lights are a group of lighting instruments that generate a stream of light waves that are parallel and close together. The light is intense, carries a good distance, and can be harsh-looking—shadows associated with this type of light are hard-edged.

Flood lights generate light that is soft-looking and perhaps flat, in that the light waves generated by floods are not parallel nor are they close together. Flood lights are harder to control than spot lights and do not carry as far or with as much intensity as spot lights. A wide variety of instruments from numerous manufacturers is available on the market, and the following listing of instruments is not exhaustive.

Illustration of Spot Light and Flood Light Beam Spreads

Spot Light

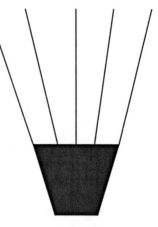

Flood Light

Spot Lights

Fresnels

The workhorse of the television studio is a spot light called a **fresnel.**
Shaped like a large tin can, fresnels are sometimes called "cans" or "aces,"
and are commonly accessorized with four black metal panels on the front
called barndoors. Fresnels come in different sizes, and the size of the can
indicates wattage—the larger the light, the higher the wattage.

A studio will commonly have at least two sizes of fresnel instruments.
The most common lighting setup would include the 1,000-watt fresnel (1K)
as the primary type of fresnel and then include a complement of lower
wattage lights (500s, 650s, or 750s). Older studios will more than likely
have a few 2,000-watt (2K) monsters in the grid—these should be handled
with care as they are quite heavy.

Fresnels are primarily used for lighting people, yet they are also commonly used for illuminating the set or creating special lighting effects.
Fresnels have focusing beams. The lamp and reflector move along an
internal track that "spots" or "floods" the lighting output.

Ellipsoidals

Another common spot light is called an **ellipsoidal.** Shaped like a long
narrow tube, ellipsoidals are sometimes called lekos, as "lekolite" was the
name given to the instrument by the manufacturer. Ellipsoidals are not
often used for illuminating people. Rather, they are an effects light often
used for sets, props, or special effects.

Ellipsoidals contain internal shutters that permit the light to be shaped
into patterns and other geometric shapes. They can also accept precut
"gobos" that can project just about any two-dimensional pattern you can
imagine (often a logo). Ellipsoidals are designed in multiple wattage setups, but are commonly 750-watt instruments.

Fresnel Spot Light

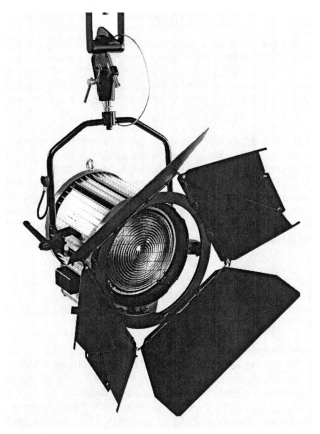

(Courtesy of ARRI.)

Flood Lights

Scoop
Flood lights are used to illuminate large areas of the studio with a soft, flat quality of light. A common flood light found in many studios is the "scoop." As the name suggests, the **scoop** looks like a large metal bowl with a lamp in the bottom. Scoops are often used for increasing the amount of base light on a set, notching up the overall illumination of a given setup.

Softlight
The **softlight** or **softbox** is perhaps the more common type of flood light in use in a modern studio. Softboxes, as the name suggests, are box-shaped lighting instruments that usually contain multiple lamps.

Three common softlights are the fluorescent, the halogen (tungsten filament), and the **cyc light.** The cyc light itself comes in a few variations—the **ground row** (a strip of lights), an individual cyc light (positioned on the ground and washing upward), or a **sky cyc** (a small softlight mounted to the grid that washes from top to bottom).

Broads
A **broad** is a flood light that contains a two-prong halogen lamp fixed between two reflectors. While the usual spot for a broad is on the grid, it is not uncommon to see a broad light floor mounted (or on tripod-like mounts).

Fixed focal length lights
Parabolic aluminum reflector lights **(PARs)** are lighting instruments that are of a "fixed" throw or spread. However, PARs are manufactured all along the continuum between spot and flood lights.

For example, PARs can be purchased as wide flood lights (WFLs) and very narrow spot lights (VNSP)—just remember, the beam spread is fixed. It is not uncommon to find PARs mounted in banks (groups) in order to create very powerful sources of light (usually on location and not in studio situations).

Fluorescent Softlight

(Courtesy of ARRI.)

Parabolic Aluminum Reflector (PAR) Light

(Courtesy of ARRI.)

Lighting Strategy

Once a set has been designed, manufactured, and constructed in the studio, a lighting strategy or design will need to be created—if it has not already been established. It is very common for a lighting strategy to be created alongside and at the same time as the set design. Often, a lighting designer is contracted for this type of work at the network affiliate level. However, the basics of lighting design are straightforward.

Two very basic and common approaches to lighting are to either follow a **three-point lighting** strategy or to pursue a "bank" or flood lighting strategy within a given setup. As the name suggests, three-point lighting utilizes three lighting instruments for each talent position on a set. The set itself and any effects lights are added only after the talent positions are taken care of. Bank lighting is altogether different. The entire set is ringed with very soft flood lights in a "bank" technique. The talent positions are merely included within the ring and the entire set will appear even (and flat and boring).

The primary advantage of three-point lighting is control. Each talent position can be adjusted without influencing the overall lighting setup. The primary advantage of bank lighting is that the talent can be blocked (or move) anywhere on the set, and look the same. Three-point lighting generally requires more lighting instruments.

Schematic of Three-Point Lighting and Bank Lighting Strategy

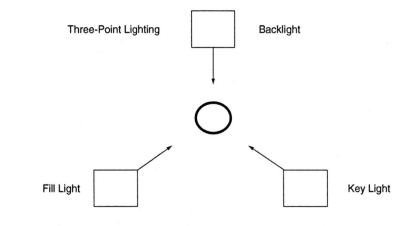

Three-Point Lighting   Backlight

Fill Light   Key Light

Bank Lighting

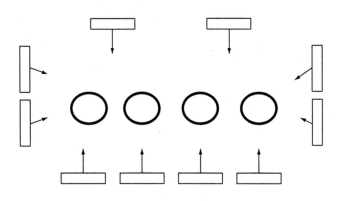

Three-Point Lighting

Key light

Each talent position on the set will be targeted with three (and sometimes more) lighting instruments. The first of these is the **key light**. The key light is located 45 degrees up, out, and to the left of the talent position. To find the location of the key light, merely sit at the talent position (precisely where the anchor is to sit) and hold your left arm straight out from your body. Then, move the arm to the left 45 degrees and up to the grid 45 degrees—the batten position you are pointing to is the location for the key light.

It is important to note that some lighting designers prefer more of a head-on key. In that case, hold the left arm straight out from your body, and merely tilt up to the grid at 45 degrees in order to locate the key position. A common instrument to use as a key light is a 1,000-watt fresnel. To aim the light, illuminate it and fully focus the lamp (spot it) to create a hot spot (an intense circle of light). Tilt and pan the instrument to bring the hot spot to rest on the left-center portion of the face of the talent.

To tune the lamp, use a **light meter** to adjust the incident light reading to a **footcandle** reading appropriate for your studio (this will depend on the type of cameras your studio is using). For example, adjust the key to 120 footcandles by defocusing (flooding) the fresnel. Once a reading of 120 footcandles is reached, adjust the **barndoors** (if equipped) on the front of the light to control **spill** (try to light only the talent).

Ellipsoidal Flood Light

(Courtesy of Altman Lighting.)

Scoop Flood Light

(Courtesy of Altman Lighting.)

Three-Point Lighting II

Fill light

The second lighting instrument in three-point lighting is the **fill light**. Two instruments are ideal for use as fill lights in a studio setup and each for entirely different reasons. A softbox will provide an excellent fill source that will not overpower the key light. However, a softbox cannot be tuned as precisely as a fresnel without moving the lighting instrument (or the talent). A key light matched (1,000-watt) or lesser wattage fresnel can be used to good effect as a fill light. Diffusion material can be used to soften the light if desired.

The fill light is placed 45 degrees up, out, and to the right of the talent position. To find the location of the fill light, merely sit at the talent position (precisely where the anchor is to sit) and hold your right arm straight out from your body. Then, move the arm to the right 45 degrees and up to the grid 45 degrees—the batten position you are pointing to is the location for the fill light.

After hanging the light in position, focus the light to a hot spot and aim the spot to the right-center of the talent's face. Tune and barndoor the light following the procedure outlined for the key light. If a softbox or other flood light is to be used, carefully aim the light to encompass the right-center portion of the talent's face. Move the instrument away from or closer to the talent while using a light meter to attempt to match (or read slightly under) the footcandle level of the key light.

Backlight

Once the key and fill lights have been hung, aimed, and tuned, the third lighting instrument in the three-point setup needs attention—the **backlight**. The backlight is located 45 degrees above and 90 degrees straight back from the talent position. A lower wattage fresnel is a good choice for the backlight (if the key is 1K, the backlight is ideal at 500 watts).

Hang the lamp in position, aim the hot spot at the shoulder-blade level of the talent, and tune the lamp to match or read slightly under the key light (tuning the backlight need not be a precise exercise as it will not affect flesh tone). The backlight creates a visual separation of the talent from the background, creating depth and interest. More lights can be added at this point (hair lights, kickers, side lights) although all are for effect rather than primary illumination. Hair lights, for example, can provide an extra accent of light that can improve the look of the talent.

Three-Point Lighting

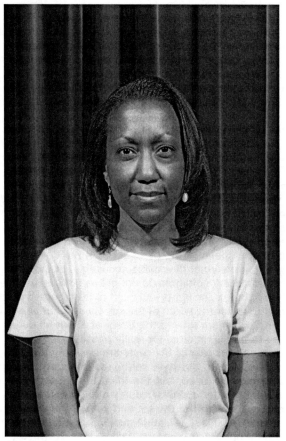

(Courtesy of Martin Seymour.)

Flood Lighting

The next lighting strategy is quick, efficient, and highly flexible. However, the "look" achieved by using a ring of flood lights to illuminate a news set may not be as appealing as that of the three-point strategy.

To begin the process, imagine a circle on the studio floor that encompasses the news set. From that imaginary circle on the floor, extrapolate the circle to the lighting grid at a 45-degree angle. The general placements of the lighting instruments will be along the imaginary line created on the grid.

The areas of placement that will need the most attention will be the front of the circle (the key lights for the talent) and the rear of the circle (the back lights). Although old-style softboxes (halogen), scoops, or other flood lighting may be used, the only flood lights that work well in the front portion will be fluorescent softboxes (like those made by Balcar).

The working distance is close (10 to 15 feet at about 55 degrees), so the lighting instruments are often mounted on telescoping poles. The lights along the front of the set should be mounted equidistant from each talent position (which may necessitate more of a straight-line approach depending on the shape of the news set). On the downside, fluorescent softlights are generally not dimmable, focusable, or easily controlled. On the upside, fluorescent softlights do not get as hot and use less electricity than halogen lighting. The lights will need to be mounted in the row wide enough apart to cover the width of the set. Hang them about 10 to 15 feet out, angle and aim them toward the talent at about 55 degrees, and turn them on—no tuning is required (or really possible).

The lights along the rear of the circle are basically functioning as back-lights or **kickers.** Again, old-style softboxes (halogen), scoops, or other flood lighting may be used, but the ideal is to match the instruments used in the front to offer a similar quality of light across the set. Mount a row that covers the width of the set and yet is high enough to avoid an unwanted cameo. At this point, additional lighting banks can be added to the left and right portions of the layout circle if so desired.

Broad Flood Light

(Courtesy of Altman Lighting.)

Softbox

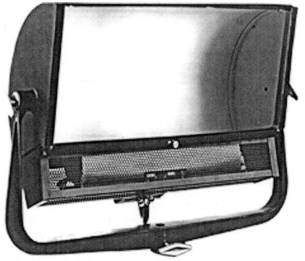

(Courtesy of Altman Lighting.)

Lighting a Chroma Key Wall

The chroma key wall must be lit evenly for the key effect to work well. Newer technology (Ultimatte and the like) in keying is much more forgiving, but nonetheless a smooth lighting job will make the weather forecast appear clean.

Begin by lighting the chroma key wall with fluorescent softboxes (like Balcars), three or more grid-mounted cyc lights, or halogen softboxes. The downward wash effect should be such that nearly all of the light is on the chroma key wall or cyc and is well contained in the immediate floor area where the two meet. The light should be even, smooth, and not so intense as to make the wall appear white (color is critical).

One technique you can use to light the area where the weather anchor will deliver the forecast is to begin by marking a parallel line to the cyc or wall about 4 to 5 feet out from the wall. The line should extend the entire width of the chroma key wall or cyc that will be in use. The weather anchor will walk back and forth along this line and needs to be well lit at all points along it.

From a centered, standing position, hold both arms straight out from your body. Move them up to the grid at a 45-degree angle. Now, begin to separate your arms to about 55 degrees—the spots you are pointing to mark the light placements. Hang low-wattage fresnels with diffusion in each position (or diffused broads with barndoors). Unfocus each (that is, fully flood) in order to permit the entire line of action to be covered. Use the barndoors to sharply control any spill on the chroma key wall.

Each of these lights really functions as a fill light, and a key will need to be added. The key in this situation will need to be head on (90 degrees) and at a steep enough angle so as to not interfere with (throw a shadow on) the chroma key wall. The choice of light is crucial. A good technique is to use a small, highly diffused broad with barndoors or a softbox as the key. Lighting a chroma key wall is 50 percent art and 50 percent science, and experimentation will be required to get the best result for your particular setup.

Effects lighting

After lighting the talent, any other lighting is for effect. Common lights will illuminate the flat wall or background curtain (cyc lights and grid-mounted softboxes are good choices). Ellipsoidals can be used to accent the front of the news desk or a station logo. Take care not to overlight your set—the use of too many effects lights will distract from the content of the news program and may suggest more of a game show feel to your viewers.

Chroma Key Wall

(Courtesy of Martin Seymour.)

Studio Cameras
and Floor Directing

Introduction

The following chapter describes two common technical production assignments in the studio. The jobs are fairly straightforward. **Studio Camera** is the person assigned to operate the studio television camera. In many studios, each camera will have an operator. However, a definite trend in studio-based camera work is the appearance of robotic and remote-controlled cameras. Not all studios, therefore, will hire a Camera Operator for each camera. Often, one person can control all of the camera units with a joystick and a computer.

The **Floor Director** (or Floor Manager), on the other hand, is the technical "boss" of the studio. The best Floor Directors are knowledgeable about all of the other technical jobs in the studio so that they may assist others if needed. The Floor Director's primary job is to communicate with the talent. The Floor Director also operates/functions as the eyes, ears, and mouth of the Director to some extent. Studio safety can be another responsibility of the Floor Director. When a show is live, or is in production, the Floor Director is the ultimate authority in the studio.

Studio Camera

The person assigned to the Studio Camera position is responsible for operating the studio camera unit. The usual protocol during production is to refer to the position by camera number, rather than operator name, so the camera number becomes a proper name of sorts: "Camera One, come help me coil this cable," or "Camera One is in the bathroom and will return shortly."

The job begins before the show starts. The operator will need to deploy the camera first. Preparing to move a camera and rolling it across a studio floor is not as simple as it may appear. Camera units are heavy, tethered to the control room through a patch panel via a thick **camera cable**, locked into position with at least five separate locking mechanisms, and are expensive ($30,000 per unit is "average").

If the camera unit is "parked" along the studio wall (as they often are), the operator will need to "unlock" the wheels first (three wheels, three locks). The **wheel lock** prevents the wheel from moving. On some units, wheel locks are sistered with directional locks that lock the wheels in a particular direction.

The operator unlocks the wheels and moves the camera away from its parking spot, taking care not to put undo stress on the camera cable. Camera cables are commonly spooled like a garden hose on the studio wall or in a figure-eight wrapped on the studio floor.

Drive safely

Often, it is good form to have one person deal with the cable while another person "drives" the camera to position. The appropriate spot from which to grab, push, and steer the camera is the "steering wheel."

While "driving" a camera, take care not to run over any cables, equipment, or people. Drive slowly—it is possible to "wreck" a camera just as one wrecks a car. Once the camera is in position, the Camera Operator will need to unlock the rest of the camera unit and begin a sequence of tasks to power up and tune the camera.

Studio Television Camera

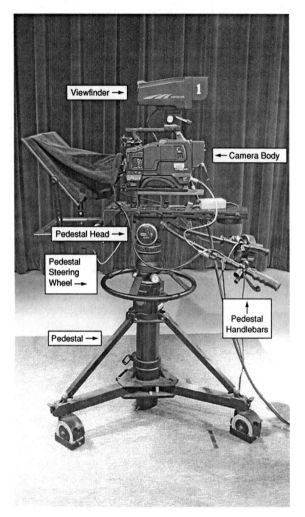

Viewfinder →

1

← Camera Body

Pedestal Head →

Pedestal
Steering
Wheel →

Pedestal
Handlebars

Pedestal →

Unlock the Locks

Just about all studio camera units will have a pedestal or **column lock** that prevents the camera from moving up and down. The lock may be colored red or labeled in some other fashion, but once it is located, it will need to be released. If the lock is a knob of some kind, it can be released by rotating it counterclockwise (thus, to engage the lock, rotate clockwise). As the column mechanism may be under pressure, care should be exercised when initially disengaging this type of lock.

If it is a ring-type lock, you will need to push down on the camera unit, turn the ring, and release the unit. A word of caution: some camera units have both types of locks. The pedestal or column lock is released when the operator can move the entire camera unit up and down freely and smoothly. The camera should be positioned at a comfortable height for the operator as well as provide an eye-level view of the talent.

On the pedestal head, two more locks are common—the **tilt lock** and the **pan lock**. Again, the manufacturer may have color-coded the locks to ease identification, but they must be located and disengaged before the unit can be used properly. The tilt lock and pan lock are usually knob-type locks but they vary by manufacturer (some look like levers)—to disengage the locks, rotate the knob (or lever) counterclockwise.

The pan lock has been released when the camera pivots freely from left to right. The tilt lock has been released when the camera pivots freely to "look" up or "look" down. One more lock may be present—the **master lock**. Not all units will have it. If the operator has released the tilt lock and the unit will not pivot, a master lock is present. Usually, it is a large, spring-loaded pin that is located "through" the pedestal head (traveling from left to right). In order to release it, locate the "head" of the pin, pull the pin out from the head and twist it so that it will hold open. The camera should now tilt freely. (To relock a master lock of this type, turn the head of the pin and allow the pin to "slip" back through the head. Careful—this one is a common finger-eater.)

The camera unit is fully unlocked when it can roll in any direction, move up and down, pivot left and right, and pivot up and down. The protocol for any given studio will vary, but it is good form to re-engage the tilt lock when leaving the camera unattended (even for a moment) while it is deployed.

Column Lock

Pan Lock

Tilt Lock

Parts and Pieces

The viewfinder

The **viewfinder** on the camera shows the operator what the camera "sees." When the camera is powered up, the viewfinder will also be receiving power (there is usually no on/off switch). However, it is common to turn the brightness or contrast controls down (these are pegged counterclockwise) to prevent the monitor unit from burning in an image or wearing out prematurely.

The Camera Operator will need to adjust the viewfinder image (brightness/contrast) and the viewfinder position (it pivots and tilts). Located on the front of the viewfinder will be a **tally light**. When the tally light is "on," it means that the camera is selected to Video Program, and the camera is hot, active, or live (the one everyone is looking at). On a side note, tally lights can usually be turned off at the viewfinder as well.

Camera control unit (ccu) and power

The camera unit is operated both manually and by remote control (not to be confused with a robotic pedestal). The remote control for the camera is called the **camera control unit (CCU)**. The CCU is commonly located in the control room and is operated by the Broadcast Engineer.

The camera is usually powered by remote (as opposed to battery power or an independent AC/DC unit). However, the operator in the studio will need to "tell the camera" how it is to be powered. The power indicator switch will need to be properly set to CCU and the power switch will need to be set to the "on" position.

It is important to note that specific studio cameras will vary widely by manufacturer. Each studio will be slightly different in its camera configuration and the protocols for powering up a camera unit will also vary. Once the camera is powered up, the **charge-coupled devices (CCDs)**—the internal imaging chips—will need to be tuned and balanced with the other cameras through the CCUs. The Broadcast Engineer will white-balance the cameras and adjust how the cameras "see" specific colors and "view" contrast.

Prompter power and input

The teleprompter equipment mounted to the front of the camera unit will need to be powered up (if so equipped). A separate on/off switch (apart from the camera) will be located on the prompter.

Like any video monitor, the prompter unit may be able to monitor multiple video inputs. Therefore, the Camera Operator will need to ensure the unit is switched to the appropriate input.

Viewfinder with Tally Light

Studio Camera Teleprompter

(Courtesy of Listec.)

Intercom

Headset, beltpack, and XLR cable

Once the camera is ready to go, the Camera Operator will need to locate an **intercom unit** in order to communicate with the control room and the rest of the production crew. The basic intercom unit has three parts: the **headset,** the **beltpack,** and an **XLR cable** of some length that will hook into the patch panel.

The headset is connected to the beltpack. The beltpack is connected to the patch panel with the XLR cable. It is important to note that some camera units have the beltpack built into the camera body. If this is the case, the headset will plug into the camera and no beltpack or XLR is needed.

It is common to operate a two-channel intercom system so that the Director can isolate certain crew members on a particular channel. The Camera Operator will need to know what channel(s) to monitor on the intercom and make volume adjustments for the headphone portion of the headset—both controls are located on the beltpack (or on the camera body itself).

The final control on the beltpack adjusts the microphone of the headset. Usually, a button can be pressed to activate the microphone. When the button is released, the microphone will go dead. To keep the microphone active (on some beltpacks), press the button twice (quickly) and the microphone should stay "on." Similar microphone controls (often a three-position toggle-type switch) are located on the camera body if the beltpack is built in.

A Typical Intercom Unit—Headset, Beltpack, and XLR Cable

Camera Operations

Set the drag/friction controls

Located near the pan lock and tilt lock on most professional pedestals, the Camera Operator will find controls for pan drag/friction and tilt drag/friction. Drag or friction is the relative resistance the pedestal head will give when a Camera Operator attempts to pan, or alternately, attempts to tilt.

The correct adjustment for drag depends on the weight of the camera, the type of pedestal head, and the preference of the operator. A correctly adjusted setup will permit the Camera Operator to make camera moves smoothly.

Set focus

At the point that production commences, the Camera Operator will need to anticipate and respond to commands from the Director. However, certain operations will need to be performed without a specific direction to do so. For example, the Camera Operator will need to "set focus." To do this, the Camera Operator will zoom in as far as possible to the target (usually an anchor's eye—it has a lot of detail). The Camera Operator will then adjust the focus control to get the crispest image possible. (If the anchor is not available, try the edge of the anchor's chair.)

Once the focus is "set," the Camera Operator can zoom out to the framing that is appropriate for the needs of the program. As long as the camera does not move toward or away from the target (or as long as the target does not move), the focus should remain correct through the range of the zoom. The Camera Operator is an image provider and creator—he or she should have (as much as possible) a usable shot for the Director to select when needed.

The Camera Operator may use a **shot sheet** (a list of shots) as a reminder of the progression and sequence of compositions needed for a given program. Again, it is important for the Camera Operator to anticipate the Director, and not merely react to directing commands. When a Director does give a command, the Camera Operator should comply as quickly and as smoothly as possible—the Camera Operator also needs to know (at all times) if the camera he or she is operating is the active program source.

Shot Sheet

CAMERA ONE

RUN#	DESCRIPTION
105	CENTERED 2 SHOT
115	SINGLE SHOT LEFT (KEY SHOT)
125	SAME
145	CHROMA KEY WALL (WX)
225	SINGLE SHOT RIGHT (CENTERED)

Camera Commands

Pan, tilt, dolly (or track), truck (or crab)
Common commands begin with the Director identifying the camera by number and then specifying the desired action. For example, the Director might say, "Camera One, set focus and reset your shot." Other common commands include: pan, tilt, dolly, truck, center or center-up, and zoom.

A **pan** command indicates a pivoting move to the left or to the right; if the Director says, "pan right," he or she is basically saying "show me what is to the right." A **tilt** command is also a pivoting move—either up or down.

A **dolly** (or **track**) command means moving the entire camera unit forward or backward: "Camera One, dolly-in" or "dolly-out," as the case may be. A **truck** (or **crab**) command is an indication to move the entire unit left or right.

During any move, the Camera Operator should maintain a consistent and average speed. Do not halt a move until the Director indicates—you don't want a Director saying, "Camera One, pan right," then "a little more ... a bit more." A centering command indicates the Director wants the target (maybe the anchor's head) centered on the screen.

Zoom
Zoom commands indicate the desire to "zoom in" or "zoom out" as the case may be. To activate a zoom, locate the zoom control. The zoom control is a thumb lever that you press to the right (to zoom in) or to the left (to zoom out). Although newer zoom controllers have speed dials that can be preset, operators should be aware that many are pressure sensitive—the harder you hit it, the faster the zoom.

Focus knob and zoom control location
In the United States, the protocol is to locate the focus knob on the left stick of the pedestal and to mount the zoom control on the right stick. In the United Kingdom, the protocol is reversed.

Trucking and Dollying

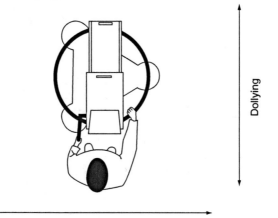

Dollying

Trucking

Camera Tips

The requirements of the Camera Operator position are different for every show and every Director, and will vary from studio to studio. The Camera Operator will need to become highly proficient in the use of the studio camera in order to be of value to the Director. The operator will need to be flexible—able to capture/acquire professional quality images while responding to the technical requirements of the camera itself.

A few tips are warranted: anticipate the Director (stay one step ahead of what the Director will need); begin and end each camera move with a decent composition (start a move on a good shot and end on a well-composed shot); be consistent and smooth (the speed of a zoom or the speed of a move should be consistent from beginning to end); the Director should never have to issue a command twice (listen well); and, never use the intercom system as your own personal walkie-talkie (not only is it really poor form, when the Director speaks, the crew listens).

When the program is completed, the Camera Operator is responsible for striking the camera unit. The unit will need to be powered down, the viewfinder dimmed, the camera cable must be recoiled or wrapped, and the camera will need to be reparked and entirely locked down. Finally, the intercom unit must be properly stowed.

Composition tips

Headroom

Headroom is the visual distance from the top of the talent's head to the top edge of the video monitor. Too much headroom means that visually, there is too much space between the talent's head and the top of the picture. Although it is uncommon, it is possible to have too little headroom. The choice is an artistic one that will need to be negotiated between the Director and the Camera Operator.

Leadroom

Leadroom is the visual distance in front of a moving object (like a car passing by) or in front of a visual composition of a person's head. If the talent on camera is looking to the right or the left, "room to look into" should be provided.

Headroom

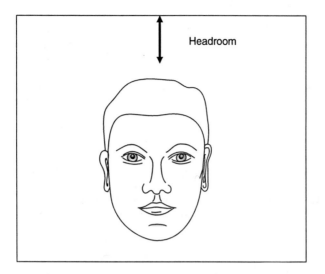

Headroom

Leadroom

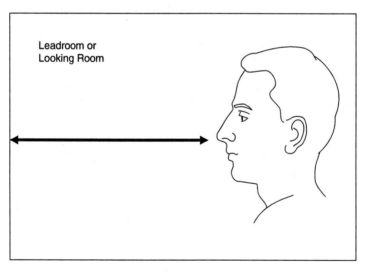

Leadroom or
Looking Room

Floor Directing

The Floor Director (or Floor Manager) is the senior production staff position in the studio. While the Floor Director's primary responsibility is to work with the talent, the job often requires rendering assistance to Camera Operators, Gaffers, Audio Technicians, and others who work in the studio environment. The most effective Floor Directors to work with, it follows, are ones who have "worked their way up" through the other studio positions first.

A Floor Director is like an in-studio representative of the Director. He or she relays commands from the Director to the entire studio staff—some of these will be audible, and some will be "translated" into hand gestures. The Floor Director also is responsible for communicating with the anchors on set—for cuing the anchors—and for assisting the anchors with the technical requirements of the television studio. The Floor Director is also responsible for "hosting" any guests in the studio that may be part of a given program.

The Floor Director in pre-production
Prior to the beginning of the program, the Floor Director will review the rundown of the show (an outline of the events of the program) in order to identify any major technical changes that have been planned for that particular broadcast. Television programs follow fairly specific technical recipes in order to reduce confusion among the production crew. For example, the newscast may always begin with a dollying reverse-zoom on Camera Two and a dissolve to Camera One for the introduction of the first story. Another example might concern tape operations—such as always beginning with VTR A at the top of a block.

Any major changes to the rundown will need to be identified and sorted out among the production crew. The Floor Director will take the lead on communicating these changes to the studio staff—including the anchors.

Prior to the show, the Floor Director will need to prepare an intercom setup (as described above) in order to communicate with the control room and the rest of the production crew. The Floor Director will pre-check to be sure the lighting grid is powered up properly (and may assist a Lighting Director in changing out bulbs if needed). Also, although many anchors prefer to "dress" their own microphones, it is not uncommon (and is sometimes expected) that the Floor Director will assist with this task as well.

The Camera Operator and the Director

The directing commands that a Camera Operator must respond to are numerous. However, a good Director will always give a "ready" cue and a "do it" cue of some kind. A good Director will also not force a Camera Operator to make complicated camera moves while the camera is in program mode. Consider the following examples:

Example One:

Director says, "Camera One set focus."

Camera One operator engages zoom control until "pegged" (zoomed in as far as possible) on the target (ideally the eye of the talent). Camera Operator will turn focus control knob until image is crisp and re-engage the zoom (out) to proper/desired framing.

Example Two:

Director says, "Camera One pan left."

Camera One operator pushes against the pedestal sticks to his or her right (thus pivoting the camera lens to the left). A distinct start to the move and consistent speed of the move is ideal.

Director says, "Hold."

Camera One operator ceases the move.

Example Three:

Director says, "Camera One needs more headroom."

Camera One operator will tilt up by pushing down on the pedestal sticks (thus pivoting the camera lens upward).

Director says, "Hold."

Camera One operator ceases the move and holds the framing.

Microphones and Sound Check

Microphone placement

The procedure for proper microphone placement is determined, to some extent, by what the anchor happens to be wearing that day. The primary objective is to mount the microphone unobtrusively, yet close enough to the mouth of the talent to get a strong audio signal. An easy rule to follow uses the distance between the thumb and pinky (with the hand spread out), where the thumb is placed on the anchor's chin (anchor head is level) and the hand is rotated so that the pinky points to a spot on the chest of the talent. A mic placement in this general area (horizontally) should be adequate to acquire a good signal.

The second objective is to "dress" the cable that connects the microphone head to the microphone power pack. Often, this will require the talent to drop the power pack down the back (or front) of the shirt—the microphone head can then "sneak" between shirt-front buttons to ride on a lapel or tie—or to mount it on the collar. In any case, the cable between the microphone head and microphone power pack should be barely seen. The power pack should be mounted on a belt, pocket, or on the belt line of the pants (to the rear is best).

At this point, the Floor Director should be sure to turn the microphone power pack "on." If the mics are wireless, the signal should now be transmitting to the audio area in the control room. If the mics are not wireless, they will need to be connected to the appropriate patch panel via an XLR cable or hooked into an audio snake at the designated terminal.

Sound check

Once the microphones are hooked up, the Floor Director will often assist the Audio Technician with microphone checks for each microphone to be used in the show. Since it is rare to have an Audio Technician in the studio during the program, the Floor Director should be prepared to solve any audio difficulties that might arise during a show. The Floor Director should have ready access to replacement microphones, batteries, and XLR cables in case instant troubleshooting is required.

A Properly Mounted Lavaliere Microphone

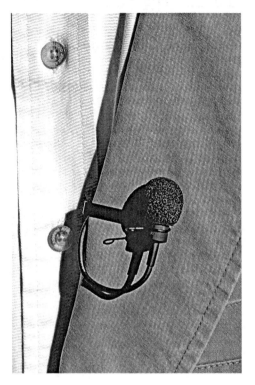

Floor Directing the Studio Staff

Communicate

Once the talent is miked, seated, and the mic checks have been completed, it is good form for the talent to remain in position for the rest of the program. Therefore, it is not uncommon for the talent to request water (or other items) from the Floor Director. While this "gophering" is usually not a problem in a professional environment, the talent should be careful not to abuse the privilege, and Floor Directors should take care not to encourage the behavior.

Once the talent is in position on the set, the Floor Director should be sure to discuss any technical changes in the rundown or other blocking changes that are planned with the entire studio staff. The communication between the Floor Director and the anchors needs to be effective. Have you ever seen an anchor looking at the wrong camera? Well, the person responsible was more than likely the Floor Director.

In any production situation, the communication protocols between the Floor Director and the talent must be worked out in advance. The Floor Director, to some extent, helps to make the anchors look good. By filtering and translating the headset chatter, the Floor Director keeps the communication in the studio efficient, calm, and on point.

Cuing talent, cuing the studio crew

The cues that a Floor Director gives will either be audible "echoes" of the Director or Assistant Director or "translated" into silent hand signals/gestures. The choice of cue is determined by the status of the microphones—if the mics are hot, the cues will be silent; if the mics are off, the cues can be audible.

Cues need to be easily seen or heard by the crew, given quickly and efficiently, and must not interfere with the production. There is no need to give cues while crouching in front of a camera. The Floor Director should stand to the side of the active camera (the camera in program) or next to the immediate following camera (the camera in preview).

The hands of the Floor Director should never pass in front of the camera lens, nor should cues be given forward of the lens itself (this includes below-the-lens cues). Generally, cues are fairly standardized in the industry, and the cues described on the next page are some of the more common you may encounter.

Chart of Common Floor Director Signals

The Floor Director and the Director

Responding to Time Cues

Floor Director Will Say:	Floor Director Will Show:
"1 minute"	one finger
"30 seconds"	crossed arms or C-shaped hand
"15 seconds"	fist
"stand by"	full hand, palm out, fingers up

Responding to Commands from the Director

Floor Director Hears:	Floor Director Will:
"cue"	swing from "stand by" downward toward the talent
"wrap"	hand/fist/finger "rotates" in the air
"cut"	finger "cuts" across neck
"stretch"	hands "pull" imaginary taffy
"ready to swing"	arms out with both hands "pointing" at active camera
"swing"	both hands "sweep" toward incoming camera
"take"	arms out, both hands "pointing" at new active camera

Prompter, Graphics, Tape

Introduction

The following chapter describes crew positions that are usually located in the control room. As such, the jobs are somewhat constrained by the particular installation in any given television station. For example, the procedures associated with the **Graphics** position will vary a great deal depending on the software package used to create and manage the graphics required for the show. Nonetheless, certain common tasks and procedures are associated with these jobs.

This chapter also describes two fairly common and complex special effects—digital video effects (DVE) and keying. Again, depending on how the control room is set up, these tasks can be handled by the Technical Director or the Graphics position. The use of **electronic still-store (ESS)** in the newscast is another procedure that fits into these effects tasks. It is important to remember that much of what this chapter will cover can and will vary depending on the hardware or software that has been purchased and installed. As such, some of these jobs have become rather proprietary or specialized.

Prompter

The **teleprompter** is a computer that turns the script into a scrollable graphic. Once the script is in this graphic form, it is transmitted as video to a monitor (CRT or LCD) mounted horizontally off the front of the studio camera units. The image from the monitor is projected onto a one-way mirror mounted diagonally in front of the camera lens. The lens is covered with a fabric tent to limit light flow from behind the mirror—increasing the contrast of the graphic image.

As anchors look at the camera, they thus do not see the lens. Rather, they see a flat glass mirror that is reflecting an image of the script. Prompter units are after-market camera accessories—they are purchased as add-ons to the camera units from manufacturers who specialize in these packages.

The prompter computer can be any PC that runs the operating system required by the software manufacturer. Teleprompting software usually operates like an extraordinarily basic word processing package, and the software may be tied into newsroom management software (like the AVID iNews package).

Prompters tend to operate in two modes: edit mode and prompt mode. In edit mode, scripts can be loaded manually, imported as files, saved, and edited—basically treated like any other word processing document. In prompt mode, the script becomes a scrollable graphic. Often, the control mechanism for the scroll can be handled with a mouse wheel or by using the scroll bar to the right of the document window. Other controls will be located in drop-down menus depending on the software. This might include the usual document formatting controls like color, font, size, alignment, underline, bold, and line spacing, but may also control scroll speeds and other prompting functions.

Prompter crew position

The person who operates the teleprompter computer is usually referred to as the Prompter. The job may be filled by a member of the production crew if it only requires script recall, but it is not uncommon to find a member of the producing staff in the position.

However, in a breaking news situation, or a larger metropolitan news market, the job may be best left to a writer—or other member of the producing staff. With some integrated software packages, changes can be made to the script from any networked PC after the show has commenced and the prompting function is engaged.

Thus, a producer can delete or add script on the fly—mixing the edit and prompt modes. The only requirement for operating the prompting computer in prompt mode is for the operator to carefully listen to the anchors. The speed of the scroll is never consistent—one cannot set it and forget it. The scroll speed will need to be constantly modulated based on the speech pacing of the talent.

Graphics Workspace on a Pinnacle DEKO System

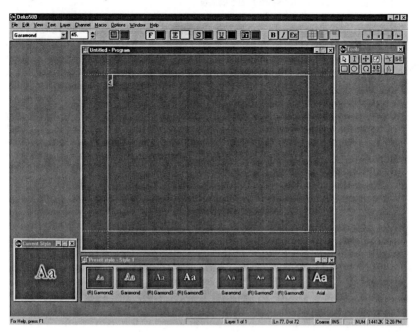

Graphics Overview

The Graphics operator for a typical newscast is usually located in the control room and is often simply named "Graphics," although this protocol may vary. The person assigned to the Graphics position operates one or more computers that create and manage the files needed for at least two functions: character generation (CG) and electronic still-store (ESS). In some cases, other functions will be added—3D modeling, or motion graphics, or animation.

Character generation (or caption generation) is the creation of text that can be keyed (layered) over another video source (like a camera shot or video clip), or, the creation of text and backgrounds that can be taken as a straight video source (like a full screen of sports scores).

ESS is the creation and management of still images and illustrations that can be keyed (layered over other video) or taken as a straight video source.

As you might imagine, CG and ESS can be combined to create multi-layered graphics that can then be saved as an entirely new and singular graphic—(imagine a picture of the Grand Canyon with the word "Grand Canyon" typed over the image). Now, you might also imagine that either element (the CG or the ESS) might be animated in some way—(the words "Grand Canyon" might fly around the screen or we might start with a close-up of a cactus and zoom out to reveal a wide shot of the canyon). Or, both items, the CG and the ESS, may animate at the same time.

Additionally, with the appearance of 3D modeling software in some newsrooms, a model can be created (a 3D ESS) that can be combined with traditional ESS, or CG animated and keyed (layered over other video), or taken as a straight video source. It is important to note that the choice of keying (or not) is up to the Technical Director—not the Graphics person.

3D Modeling on Lyric Pro

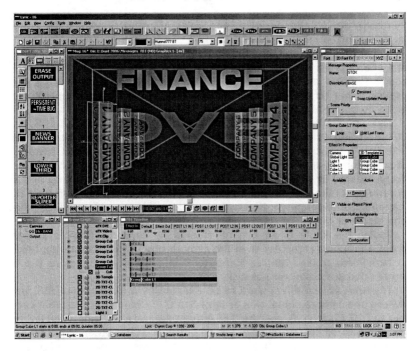

(Courtesy of Chyron.)

Digital Video Effects (DVE)

Furthermore, another wrinkle (and layer of complexity) can be added at this point—digital video effects (DVE). These can be embedded video switcher functions (and thus the domain of the Technical Director) or external effects units (smaller effects switchers) that are hooked into the main video switcher as a separate video source. External units may be controlled either by the Technical Director (TD) or the Graphics operator or even by both positions.

DVE units, prior to embedded animation functions within CG, ESS, and 3D modeling software, were originally used for some very basic effects like the "anchor box" or "split screen." The anchor box effect (where a box containing a graphic appears over the shoulder of the anchor) used to be created by assigning the ESS to the DVE (which was set up or programmed as the box shape) and then keying (layering) the DVE over the camera. Some simple motion was possible within the DVE unit (like flying the box in or out).

Today, the same effect can be created by keying a graphic straight from a graphics computer over the camera (the DVE function—the box—occurs inside of the graphics computer itself). Animation functions can be embedded in the software as well.

The split screen effect used to be enabled by a two-channel DVE unit where one camera signal was assigned to DVE Channel A, the other camera to DVE Channel B, and the DVE either taken as a straight video source to program or keyed (layered yet again) over some other video source (like a preset background). Today, the same effects can be created by activating two key layers in a separate mix effects bus (M/E) on the video switcher itself.

ESS Combined with CG

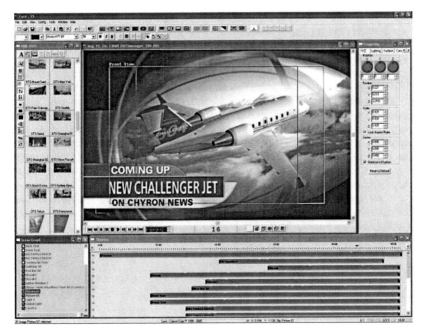

(Courtesy of Chyron.)

Keying

Yet another layer of complexity can be added to this chaos and has already been alluded to—the **key**. A key is a video layer. Any video source can be keyed over any other video source. A typical example of this is a character generation (such as a name) that is keyed over a camera shot of a person. The CG is the key—the layer. The camera shot is the background.

While this example is straightforward, consider that an animated video source (a miniature 3D dancing hippo) can also be a key source. Imagine the hippo dancing in the corner of the screen. Now consider that an animated video source (hippo) can be assigned to a DVE and the DVE assigned as the key source. The DVE is programmed to "fly" from a centered infinity point forward to fill the screen. The hippo starts very small in the center and grows to fill the screen (blocking out the camera shot).

Now consider the capability of a two-channel DVE—two separate animations flying independently over a background. Consider the fact that many switchers can handle four or more key sources at one time (five full layers of video—four key, one background—each independently controlled), and you can begin to understand the look of CNN's *Headline News*.

Example of Chroma Key

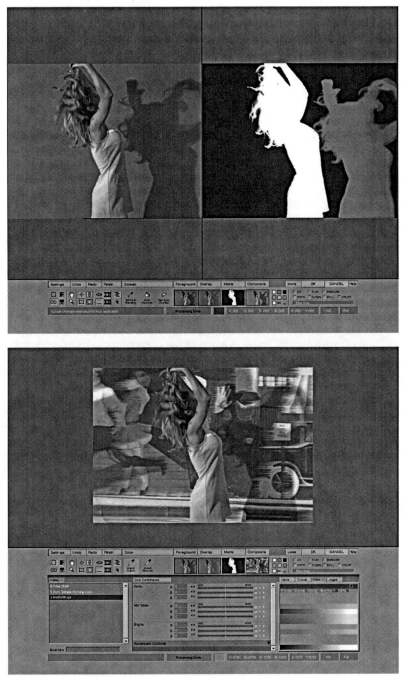

(Courtesy of Ultimatte.)

109

The Job of Graphics

Now that you are completely confused, let us return to the job and responsibilities of the crew member assigned to Graphics. For the moment, we will discuss the character generation (CG) function in isolation from the rest of what is possible in the realm of graphics.

Character generation

Remember that the CG (or CapGen) function is the creation of text—text that can be layered over (keyed) other video or taken straight. The Graphics operator will need to create the program CG—graphics that will be used every time the show airs: the anchor names (Katie Couric—CBS News), the credit roll (Wayne Nesbitt—Director), and the name of the show (*NewsWatch 44*). Each of these can be saved as independent graphics pages that can be recalled alone, or graphics can be linked together and saved in sequences of pages (like a credit roll).

Newscasts typically have a graphics format that specifies certain fonts, sizes, and colors. The format is contained in a series of electronic templates within the CG that are used to create the CG for the program.

Prior to the show, the Graphics operator will be primarily concerned with creating the CG needed to cover an individual program—the CG needed just for that particular show. Most Graphics operators have at this point already created the program CG and will merely need to load it in order into a final playlist.

The CG needed to cover an individual program, as one might imagine, will vary from show to show. Names of people, places, and reporters that appear in the video clips to be used will also need to be created, saved, and loaded (in order). One way to manage the process is to save CG files by run number and tag them in order (100-1, 100-2, 100-3, etc.).

Requests for special graphics will need to be processed and loaded—pages of sports scores, stock reports, telephone numbers to call "for more information," and the like. Once the graphics are created, each page will need to be loaded (organized) into a playlist for recall during the program. It is at this point that some software packages permit animations to be linked to particular CG pages (like flipping a name onto or off of the screen).

Graphic Output of Chyron Lyric

(Courtesy of Chyron.)

The Job of Graphics II

Electronic still-store

The ESS function of the Graphics operator is to acquire, create, and manage any still images that may be needed for a particular show. The ESS load for a news show might include but is not limited to the following: pictures of reporters (on the scene and reporting by phone), a photo of the president of the United States, an image of the Grand Canyon, the U.S. flag, Santa Claus, attack helicopters, or corporate logos.

With the advent of 3D modeling software, imaging software (Adobe Photoshop), and compositing/illustrating software, the ESS load for a news show might also include topographic maps of a coal mine, 3D models of a space craft, or a drawing of a new city plan—the list of possibilities is really endless.

In any case, each graphic can be saved independently, linked with others in a sequence, and will need to be loaded in a playlist of some fashion for recall during the program. Again, embedded animations can be linked to individual files if needed (a spinning Earth is a good example).

Combine or divide?

The Graphics position has become so complex that many news operations have attempted to manage the process by isolating and delegating graphics functions to other crew members. It is not uncommon to find the ESS function handled entirely by the TD and the CG function isolated to the Graphics operator (who would probably be referred to as "CG" instead). Often the ESS function and the CG function are handled by two separate crew members entirely apart from the TD.

Specialists in 3D modeling, animation, and compositing are often located outside of the control room entirely (in the newsroom or in a graphics department) with their sole purpose being to create complex graphics that can be recalled (played or activated) by the Graphics operator during the show.

In the case of live sports programming, multiple Graphics operators may be called upon to contribute to any given show (just imagine the graphic requirements of the Super Bowl). Once the show begins, the task of the Graphics operator is to recall the graphics in order, as needed, and on the Director's command. Not only does a Graphics operator need to be fluent in the software and creative aspects, but also the job requires a great deal of skill in organization and file management.

ESS on a Pinnacle DEKO System

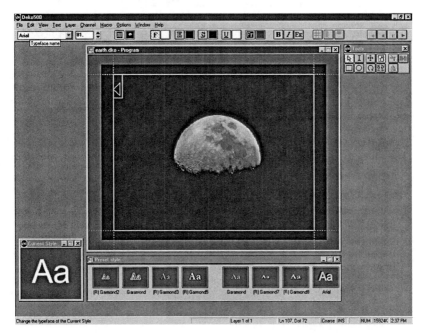

Graphics and the Director

The primary relationship between the Director and a Graphics operator is concerned with the supply of a resource (a graphic) at a specific time and on command.

The language a Director will use to call for a graphic will vary depending on the type of graphic (CG, ESS, an ESS sequence, an animation, or DVE) and the intended use—keyed or straight. Consider the following example:

Example:
The Director wishes to activate a CG (or CapGen) layer over program video.

Director says, "Stand by downstream."

The Graphics operator will have recalled the appropriate CG and it will be available in CG program as a video resource. The CG will have been prepared prior to the show in pre-production. The Technical Director will make sure the CG is selected as the appropriate key source and prepare to activate the key.

Director says, "Downstream."

The TD will activate the key.

Director says, "Ready to lose."

The TD prepares to deactivate the key.

Director says, "Lose."

The TD deactivates the key. The Graphics operator can now prepare for the next graphic.

CG on a Pinnacle DEKO System

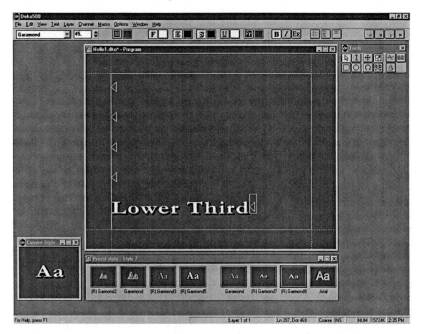

Tape

The video clips that will be shown during a newscast are the responsibility of many people—the shooters, reporters, and editors who create the clips, and the Tape operator who is responsible for actually playing them—in order, as needed, and on the Director's command. The crew member who is responsible for the video clips is called "**Tape.**"

While tape operations may be located in the control room, it is not uncommon for the physical space to be isolated elsewhere (like audio control often is) or connected in with **Master Control** (or **transmission control**) in some manner. It is also important to remember that many news operations are quickly moving to a tapeless environment, where video clips are stored and will be played from a **video server** accessed via PC.

One of the tasks associated with Tape is the actual recording of the news program. Prior to the show, Tape will need to remember to "roll record" on the show. Additionally, the Tape operator must be sure to double-check that the record video tape recorder (VTR) is receiving Video and Audio Program from the studio cleanly (and at the appropriate signal strength). However, it is not uncommon for the recording task to be delegated to Master Control.

The primary responsibility of Tape is to locate and organize the clips for playback. At least three VTRs will be utilized for playback (the use of four is good form). The VTRs will be lettered (VTR A, VTR B, etc.) in order to reduce possible communication confusion with the cameras. Each video clip will be played from one of the VTRs. Thus, a common protocol is to isolate each clip on a separate physical tape. In this way, multiple clips can be cued and ready for playback.

Tape and the Director

The directing command for rolling tape is straightforward. The Director will ready the tape, say "Stand by Tape A" and then roll the tape, "Roll Tape A."

On the ready cue, the Tape operator needs to be sure the tape is "on heads" (on pause), cued to a 3-second pre-roll (3 on the countdown), and the operator must be poised to press the play button.

On the roll cue, the Tape operator will press play and monitor the playback. As soon as the Director is finished with the clip—the VTR is no longer selected to program and the audio from the tape is no longer active—the Tape operator can eject the tape and load in the next clip that will be needed (in the meantime, the Tape operator has probably already rolled the next VTR). Remember, the average is one clip per minute—a 30-minute newscast equals 30 separate clips.

Video Clip Server

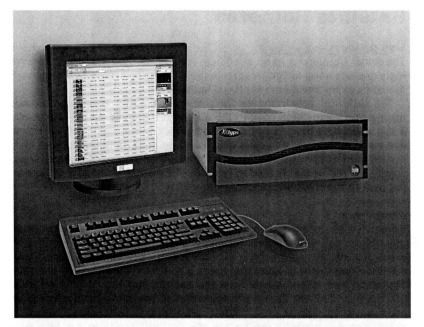

(Courtesy of Chyron.)

Live Shots, Microwave, and Satellite Remotes

Live on location

The rather ubiquitous trend in affiliate-level news operations is the seemingly endless need to "go live" from the location of a news event—even if the news event was hours (or days) in the past.

The technical requirements for getting the audio and video signals from a remote location back to the station are getting easier—especially if the news reporting is not actually live but rather "as live." An actual live remote requires an active and real-time audio and video feed from the location—this is usually accomplished via microwave or (more rarely) satellite. A report that is filed to "look live" or is handled "as live," can be fed back to the station via the Internet earlier in the news day.

Microwave

Going live on location using a microwave signal is the most common practice for the affiliate-level newscast. The process is fairly straightforward. A station-owned vehicle (usually a van or truck) is equipped with a telescoping tower (a pole) that holds a microwave transmitter antenna. The audio and video signals from the microphone and camera on location are encoded and then transmitted back to the television station using microwave technology.

The signal is typically received in Master Control where it is then separated and routed to the control room as a video source for the video switcher and an audio source for the audio console. However, it is not uncommon for the signal to be received directly in the tape area and then routed—forwarded—to the control room. Although rare, the remote signal can be received directly into the control room and hardwired as audio and video inputs.

The microwave connection

The common connection from the microwave remote truck is usually indirect (truck to a repeater [a relay] to the station). Since microwave hookups are limited as line-of-sight transmissions, repeaters are usually physically located as high as possible. Repeaters can be located on towers, mountain or hilltops, or on skyscraper roof edges (or on roof-mounted towers). The important aspect of microwave transmission to remember is that the remote truck must be able to "see" a relay for the connection back to the station to be solid. Due to these limitations, microwave links are really only feasible for local or regional reporting.

As a side note, news operations that have invested in (or leased) a helicopter are subject to the same microwave connection protocols. The signal from a helicopter, however, can be direct (helicopter to the station) since the helicopter is (hopefully) already at a height that will permit a clean "shot" back to the station. However, the signal can be indirect as well (helicopter to a relay to the station).

Schematic of Microwave Relay

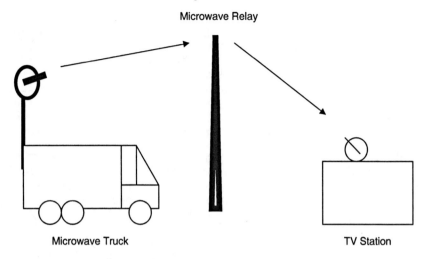

Microwave Relay

Microwave Truck

TV Station

Satellite

Going live on location using a satellite signal is a bit more complex (and expensive) than using a microwave link. However, the process is very similar to an indirect microwave connection—the relay just happens to be a satellite in space. Satellite trucks are more expensive than microwave trucks. Newer satellite units are portable (and can fit in a few equipment cases). However, a satellite system will permit live news reporting from just about anywhere on the planet. Satellite systems are also useful in news markets that are geographically difficult or extend beyond the reach of a microwave system.

A satellite signal will almost always need to be received (tuned and decoded) in Master Control before routing to the control room. Once in the control room, the audio and video feed from the satellite can be handled in the same manner as any other audio and video source.

The satellite connection
The common connection from the satellite truck (or portable unit) is indirect (truck to the satellite to the station). However, satellite hookups are limited (just like microwave is) as a line-of-sight transmission. The truck must be able to "see" the satellite and the satellite must be able to "see" the station.

Once on location, the truck will make the connection to the satellite by "leasing" the time needed for the feed from a third party who owns the satellite. Organizations such as CBS's Newspath and NBC's News Channel are designed to serve local stations by providing cost-effective satellite time, and a way to share video among the affiliated stations. Stations typically have contracts that govern the cost for time and pay a flat per-minute fee for it. The cost can be a consideration for a small-market station as satellite time can cost as much as $15 per minute with a 5-minute minimum.

Internet
The Internet has made reporting from remote geographic areas a much simpler technical task. A reporter equipped with a camera and a laptop computer can easily shoot, edit, and voice a story in the field. The segment can be incorporated into the newscast as an "as live" story.

Once the video file is completed, the file can be sent as an e-mail attachment from any reliable Internet connection (hotels make good transmission locations). As long as the file can be completely transmitted (not blocked by server protocols on file size), a compressed news package of up to 5 minutes in length can be sent through a broadband connection in less than 30 minutes. A more modest connection can be used as long as the integrity of the connection can be maintained—although it may take more time.

Schematic of Satellite Relay

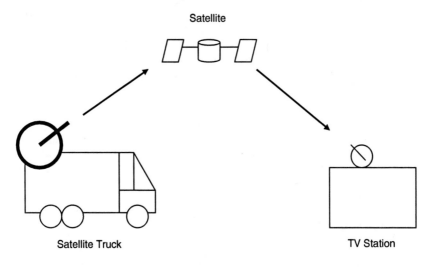

Satellite

Satellite Truck

TV Station

Directing a Live Remote

The command syntax for directing a live remote is really no different from activating any other audio and video source to program. The major worry with a remote setup is communication between the technical staff on the ground and the control room. A few procedures can be followed to help minimize the communication stress.

Program feed

First, the people on location need to be able to see and hear the output of the station—often this is handled on a return feed right through the microwave or satellite system itself. A monitor can be hooked up to serve this purpose. Additionally, an interrupt foldback (IFB) bug will need to be connected for the talent to be able to monitor program audio as well as listen to any directions from the producer.

Remote intercom

Second, the technical folks on location need to be hooked into the intercom system so that they may hear and respond to commands from the Director. Again, this can be handled on a return feed from the station. While a cellular phone connection can substitute for a true intercom connection, it is not the best choice to make.

Cellular

Third, a cell phone connection between the remote unit and the control room is a prudent communication safety measure in case the remote intercom system fails.

Rundowns, Scripts, Video Clip Information

Introduction

The process of creating any television program begins with the desire to communicate. The complex and unique visual nature of television requires the creative team to visualize the program on paper in the pre-production process.

While many tools are available to assist in the visualization process, like storyboarding, the final components that are needed for the production process include the **rundown** (or **running order**), the script, and a mechanism for conveying video clip information to the production staff.

The rundown is a segment-by-segment outline of a program. Usually formatted as a chronological list, the rundown will include information about video sourcing, audio sourcing, and timing information regarding each segment.

The script is a written document that contains the stories the anchors are to read. In multi-camera productions, the script is usually formatted in two columns with production information in the left column and the scripting in the right column. The two-column format permits the staff to track not only what the anchor is saying but also what the viewer will be seeing.

Pre-recorded video clips are a common part of most studio-based production. The clips may contain highlights of a sporting event, footage of a traffic jam, or even video of the weather. Information for each clip must be made available for the production crew regarding the location of the clip (what tape it is on, or in what computer file), the duration of the clip (how long it is), the type of clip (VO, VO/SOT, or PKG), and any graphic requirements (character generation).

The following section describes these three final components of the production process.

The Rundown

A news rundown (or running order) is a rough outline or chart indicating the technical elements required for a specific program. Everyone on the production crew should receive a copy of the rundown prior to the show. Knowing how to decipher a rundown, therefore, is important for all members of the crew.

In the most basic form, a rundown must convey the following information: segment number or identifier (RUN), the primary video source for the segment (VID), tape location if a roll-in is associated with the segment (L), the primary audio source for the segment (AUD), the segment or story slug (SLUG), the amount of time the segment is expected to run (SEG), and a total running time column for the entire program (TRT).

It is important to note that a wide variety of rundown forms are in use in the television news industry. Many rundowns are more complex than the one described here or are unique to a given program.

Segment Number (RUN)

The first column in the rundown (RUN) conveys the **segment number** or segment identifier. In the example, each segment is identified by a 100, 200, 300, or 400 series number.

Each series of numbers is called a **block** (for example, the 300 block might be identified as the "weather" segment). Each block is separated by a commercial break. Normally, there are four blocks to the half hour (although this varies), and within a block, there could be up to 99 events (101 to 199, for example). The numbering logic within a block is rarely in perfect sequence (101, 102, 103) to allow for the addition of a new segment (breaking news, for example) without requiring the entire rundown to be renumbered.

It is very common in the industry to use an alternate form of run number that uses the alphabet as block identifiers (A block, B block, C block) and numbers for specific segments (A-1, A-2, A-3). On many news programs, certain events happen every time the show airs. For example, the show teaser (indicated as run number 98) is an event that occurs every time the show airs. As such, it is a fixed item on the rundown. Run number 99, the show opener (usually a pre-produced package of video, graphics, and music), is another example of an event that is fixed ("... and now, live from Baltimore, *Eyewitness News!*").

Rundown

RUN	VID	L	AUD	SLUG	SEG	TRT
98	OC		MIC	TEASER	:20	:20
99	PKG	A	SOT	OPEN	1:10	1:30
100	OC		MIC	WELCOME	:15	1:45
105	VO	B	MIC	FIRE	:45	2:30
110	PKG	C	SOT	TRAFFIC	1:10	3:40
140	OC		MIC	HALLOWEEN	:45	4:25
145	VO/SOT	A	MIC/SOT	BOWLING	:30	4:55
199	MC	MC	MC	COMM. 1	2:00	6:55
200	OC		MIC	DESERT	:05	7:00
205	PKG	A	SOT	CANDIDATE	2:00	9:00
210	OC		MIC	INTERVIEW	5:00	14:00
299	MC	MC	MC	COMM. 2	2:00	16:00
300	OC		MIC	WX Intro.	:15	16:15
310	FX		MIC	Weather	3:45	20:00
399	MC	MC	MC	COMM. 3	2:00	22:00
400	OC		MIC	REDSOX	:30	22:30
410	PKG	A	SOT	Sup.Bowl	1:30	24:00
425	VO/SOT	B	MIC/SOT	Husky	1:30	25:30
440	PKG	C	SOT	NBA	1:00	26:30
445	OC		MIC	CLOSE	:30	27:00
450	FX		CD	Credits	1:30	28:30

Video Source (VID)

The second column on the rundown (VID) indicates the primary or dominant video source for the segment. In the example here, six types of video are identified by acronyms/initials.

OC stands for **on camera**—meaning the dominant video for the segment is to come from one of the studio cameras. In a detailed usage of OC, consider that a camera number could be easily added—OC 1, OC 2—to convey more information.

VO or **voice-over** indicates that a clip of pre-recorded video is to be the primary video source for the segment. The clip could be played back from a wide variety of specific devices (from tape, CD, DVD, or a video server) depending on the configuration of the control room one is working in (our example assumes the use of VTRs for playback).

VO, then, is a particular form of news story involving a video clip. In voice-over, the video in use for the segment will be spoken over by the anchor who is live in the studio. Usually a VO begins OC with the anchor reading an introduction and is followed by a quick roll and cut to tape for the VO portion and a cut back to camera for a concluding remark—sometimes called a **tag.**

VO/SOT (voice-over, followed by sound on tape) also indicates that a clip of pre-recorded video will be the primary video source for the segment. The VO/SOT is a close cousin to the VO, popular in sports news, and is also a form of news story.

Usually a VO/SOT begins OC with the anchor reading an introduction, followed by a quick roll and cut to tape for the VO portion (the anchor keeps reading) and then, at a pre-timed point on the tape, an edit occurs to a sound bite or SOT. The anchor stops reading, the audio will switch from the anchor to the tape, and the SOT (sound on tape) portion plays out. At the conclusion of the SOT portion of the VO/SOT, a cut back to camera for a concluding remark or "tag" from the anchor is common.

It is important to point out that VO/SOTs have many forms—the VO/SOT/VO, the SOT/VO, the SOT/VO/SOT, and so on. The concept to remember at this point is that the VO/SOT is a form of news story involving a video clip as the primary video source.

Chart of Video-Related Abbreviations

OC	ON CAMERA
VO	VOICE-OVER
VO/SOT	VOICE-OVER FOLLOWED BY SOUND ON TAPE
SOT/VO	SOUND ON TAPE FOLLOWED BY VOICE-OVER
PKG	PACKAGE
FX	GRAPHICS OR EFFECTS SEQUENCE
ESS	ELECTRONIC STILL-STORE
CG	CHARACTER GENERATOR
CAPGEN	CAPTION GENERATOR
LIVE	MICROWAVE OR SATELLITE REMOTE
MX	MICROWAVE
SAT	SATELLITE
DVE	DIGITAL VIDEO EFFECTS
MC	MASTER CONTROL
CAM	CAMERA
CAM 1	CAMERA ONE
KEY	KEY SHOT

Video Source (VID) II

PKG or **package** indicates that a clip of pre-recorded video is to be the primary video source for the segment. In this form, the video and audio are all "packaged" or produced together on the tape.

Typically, an anchor opens a PKG with a live introduction from the studio (OC), followed by a quick roll and cut to tape for the PKG. While the tape is rolling, the anchor is standing by—usually watching the package on a monitor and listening to the track on the interrupt foldback (IFB). At the conclusion of the tape, the anchor usually gives a concluding remark or tag (OC) before moving on to the next story. A common variation on the protocol is to have the anchor introduce a reporter in the field "live," and to permit the reporter to introduce the package.

Other VID

Several other acronyms or initials are commonly deployed in the VID column. As mentioned earlier in the book, CG stands for character generator—meaning the primary video source is a computer-generated text of some kind. ESS stands for electronic still-store—a picture or graphics file of some kind, also coming from a computer. FX is a generic indicator for effects or graphics, as is the abbreviation FS. Again, the most likely video source would be a control room. KEY commonly indicates an over-the-shoulder box graphic. LIVE or live inject indicates a live shot (microwave or satellite).

DVE stands for digital video effects. In DVE, a video source (or two, or three) is assigned to a special effects box that manipulates the source in some fashion. A good example of this is when two cameras are assigned to the DVE to create a split-screen effect so that reporters in different locations may seem to interact with one another on screen.

MC stands for Master Control (or transmission control). When indicated as a primary video source on a rundown, it means that the video for the segment will be handled remotely from the control room. Commercials, for example, are usually rolled from the Master Control area in the station.

Whatever the acronym or initials, remember that the VID column is all about the video source. Depending on the show, the station, or the network, a wide variety of indicators may appear in this column.

Control Room with LCD Panel Monitor Wall

(Courtesy of High Tech Furnishings.)

Location (L)

The "**L**" column conveys **location**. Historically, the column tells the reader the specific name of the VTR that houses the tape clip needed for the segment. VTRs are usually lettered (VTR-A, VTR-B) or numbered (VTR1023, VTR4092) depending on the protocol in use at the station. (Some directors prefer letters to numbers to avoid confusion with the cameras.)

So, if a segment on a rundown is to utilize a tape, a location should also be noted (this would include the VO, VO/SOT, or PKG). Likewise, if a segment utilizes no tape—an OC for instance—no location information should appear on the rundown.

The L column is taking on a new role as the control room world expands to include video clips from CD, DVD, or video servers. It is important to remember that if a pre-recorded video clip is involved with a segment, it has to come from a specific machine that can be clearly identified and easily called upon.

Audio (AUD)

The AUD column indicates the primary or dominant audio source that is in play for the segment. Like the VID column, acronyms are used to identify specific technical devices or protocols as audio sources.

MIC stands for microphone (easily expanded to convey more information—MIC 5, MIC 1). As mentioned above, SOT stands for sound on tape. The primary audio source in a SOT is the specific device shown in the location column for the segment. For example, if a PKG is in VTR-A (see Run Number 110 on page 127), the audio for the PKG portion of 110 is also VTR-A.

As shown in the example rundown, many audio sources are automatically associated with a given video source. For example, if the dominant video is OC, logically, the primary audio is MIC.

Control Room with CRT Monitor Wall

(Courtesy Grass Valley.)

Slug (SLUG)

The **SLUG** (or item) column simply indicates another identifier for the segment. A slug is a short name given to the segment by the producing staff earlier in the news day and usually prior to the final creation of the rundown. Slugs can also be merely informative—see 199 in the sample rundown on page 127, "Commercial Break #1."

A good indicator of whether a person is on the production team or on the producing staff is how that person refers to a segment. Production folks will say "we are in 105 and 110 is next." A producer might say, "we are in Fire and Traffic is next." Only major technical segments (usually a news story) get a line on the rundown. Minor or fleeting technical tasks within a story (changing from camera to tape, for example) do not typically get a separate line. If such were the case, the rundown for a typical news program would be very long indeed.

Timing (SEG and TRT)

The final two columns are for timing information. The first of these, SEG, indicates the producer's estimate as to how long the entire segment will take. SEG time is inclusive of anchor introductions, video clips, and tags (if any). So, if a video clip associated with a segment is 15 seconds long, one must add the introduction time and tag time to the clip time to figure out SEG time.

For example, if the introduction will take 5 seconds, the tape 15 seconds, and the tag 10 seconds, the SEG time would be :30.

The final column, **TRT,** stands for **total running time** for the program. TRT will be indicated in one of two forms, either additive or subtractive. Additive TRT, as is used here, begins at zero and merely adds SEG time at each line. Subtractive TRT begins with the expected total length of the program and subtracts each SEG in sequence (for example, 30:00 minus :10 is 29:50 minus 1:30 is 28:20, and so on).

The form of TRT really depends on the protocols in play at your facility. TRT is vital to the Assistant Director (AD) and the Producer. At the end of every segment, using TRT and a master clock, one can figure if the show is running long (too much material and/or too slow) or short (not enough material and/or too fast).

Newsroom software suites, like Avid's iNews, often build in a timing function that will handle total running time.

A Control Room in Production

(Courtesy Paul Neuman.)

Reading Is Fundamental

The ability to decipher a rundown is vital to all members of the production crew. While the basic form conveyed here should more than suffice to begin your rundown literacy, you should be encouraged to seek out and learn about other forms that are in use or common to a particular genre of program. No one form of rundown is the "correct" one. The important point to remember is that a rundown needs to communicate, clearly, the technical requirements of the program to the crew.

Scripting

Scripting is a producing function—writing—that has a good deal of impact on how a Director actually cues a program. The standard format for news is a two-column script. The first column indicates production information. The right-hand column is where the actual script (what the anchors will say) is located. The organization protocol for the script will follow the protocol of the rundown.

As a news show is created, the script is written, and the show is visualized by the producing staff—not only what the viewer will hear but also what the viewer will see is determined. The script, therefore, needs to reflect both.

Integrated newsroom software, like Avid's iNews, is a useful tool in creating the rundown and the script at the same time. Multiple users (writers, reporters, producers) can access all of the scripts from any newsroom computer to make changes in the running order, edits, or to add information. As will be shown in the next chapter, the script will become the primary tool that the Director will use to "call" or "cue" the program.

A Page of Script from a News Program in the Two-Column Format

120—Figure Skating

CAM 3

Olympic Gold Medalist Alexei Yaguden (AH LEX AY YAH GOO DEN) is coming to perform this weekend at Eastern Connecticut State University.

TAKE VO

:32

Yaguden, the 2002 Olympic Gold Medalist, is on tour in North America for the next year in the attempt to raise money for the Struggling Russian Gymnastics program. Yaguden, who is married to the Russian figure skating champion Bakarov (BAHK R OFF), is also trying to raise money for the other Russian teams that are also facing shortfalls. The Russian government, once well known for its support of Olympic athletes, has, in recent years, cut off all funding to the teams. Numerous athletes from the former Soviet Union have immigrated to other countries in search of financial support for training. Most have landed in the U.S., although the athletes continue to compete for Russia.

###

Video Clip Information

On average, a separate video clip will be rolled into a news program every minute. Technical information concerning each clip needs to be conveyed to the production crew in an efficient and logical manner. However, of all the "ways of doing things" in the industry, none is more varied than the vehicle for communicating video clip information to the staff.

No matter what technique is utilized, the following information regarding each clip needs to be conveyed. Beyond the basics—what show, what day, what time—one of the first items to consider is to what story or production segment (run number) is the clip associated with. What is the precise length of the clip? What kind of audio is on the clip? Do graphics need to be created to be layered over the clip? If so, what are they and precisely when in the duration of the clip are they to be layered (or keyed) over? What kind of story form is the clip (VO, VO/SOT, PKG)? If the clip is on a physical tape, what tape is the clip located on? And finally, where on that tape is the clip located? Remember that the last two items may be replaced by similar information corresponding to a file on a video server.

Student Anchors on Set

(Courtesy Paul Neuman.)

Font Sheet or Clip Sheet

One technique to convey clip information is to consolidate it onto one form—a **font sheet** (or **clip sheet**)—or some similar document. The document may be in hard copy form, accessible on a network, or both.

If you look over the example provided on page 141, you will notice that the top third of the form concerns show, tape, and clip information— including total running time (TRT). The middle third of the form is primarily designed to convey information concerning the type of clip and the timing of the clip elements. Finally, the bottom third is where graphics information (graphics associated with a video clip) can be timed and written out.

The top

The top third of the font sheet begins with a space for the run number— the segment identifier that the video clip belongs to. The date, slug, and producer are self-explanatory.

The **tape number** information refers to an identifying number that has been assigned to a physical tape in the television station. Often, this number may contain four or more digits (#1057 or #10578), according to the tape logistics (the protocol) of that station. For example, a four-digit numbering system permits containment of 9,999 physical tapes, a five-digit numbering system accommodates 99,999 physical tapes, and so on.

The **cut number** refers to a specific clip on the identified tape. Since most video clips for television news rarely exceed 3 minutes, many clips are loaded (or edited) onto any specific tape (sometimes these tapes are called edit masters). For example, a tape number of 1010 and a clip number of 7 indicate that the desired clip is on tape 1010 and is the seventh clip on the tape.

The next line provides space to indicate the presence of **natural sound (NAT)** or **atmosphere (ATMOS),** if any. If the clip has NAT (natural sound) isolated onto a specific audio channel, it will be indicated here.

TRT with PAD provides space for the **total running time** of the clip, including PAD. **PAD** is extra material on the end of the video clip that is present but is not really intended for use.

For example, suppose a story concerning holiday traffic is to air. A Producer might use some stock footage of a traffic jam to illustrate the story. If the traffic jam clip is 1 minute and the script for the story will only take the anchor 20 seconds to read, you have a situation where the clip has 40 seconds of PAD – extra material that is not really needed, but present.

Directors and Assistant Directors can use that extra time to smooth out or ease the transition from the clip back to the studio.

Font Sheet or Clip Sheet

RUN #:_____ DATE:_____

SLUG:_____ TAPE #:_____

PRODUCER:_____ CUT #:_____

NATSOUND (circle): CH1 CH2   TRT with PAD:_____

****

Story Type: VO   VO/SOT   SOT/VO   VO/SOT/VO   SOT/VO/SOT   PKG
(circle)

                SEG. TIME

VO   _____

PKG/SOT   _____   OUTCUE:_____

VO   _____

SOT   _____   OUTCUE:_____

****

TIME   FONT

_____   _____

_____   _____

_____   _____

_____   _____

_____   _____

_____   _____

141

Font Sheet or Clip Sheet II

The middle

The middle portion of the font sheet is redundant, to some extent, with portions of the rundown. Although it is provided in this example font sheet, the rundown also would indicate the story type in the VID column.

Seg

Time refers to segment time within a clip. If the clip is a VO (and only a VO), one would expect a time to be indicated to the right of the VO indicator. If the clip is a PKG (and only a PKG), one would expect a time to be indicated to the right of the PKG indicator (and so on).

However, suppose a clip is a VO/SOT. The specific length of the VO portion and the exact time of the SOT need to be conveyed. Both indicators, in this instance, would contain time information. A common protocol and variation on this is to convey time information in the body of the script.

The space to indicate an **outcue** (or **outwords**) applies primarily to packages or VO/SOT variations that end in SOT. The outcue is the last thing heard (or seen) at the end of the video clip. Knowing the outcue permits the Director (and the rest of the crew) to transition out of a tape clip as tightly as possible. It is not uncommon to see the word "standard" (or STD) written in as an outcue. A standard outcue is merely the reporter's name and station identification: "I'm Matthew Evans, CBS News."

Hosts on Interview Set

(Courtesy Martin Seymour.)

Font Sheet or Clip Sheet III

The bottom

If the clip requires character generation to be keyed over live (and most news clips do), the content of that CG and the expected time it is needed can be conveyed similarly to what is shown on the bottom of the example font sheet.

The time indicator would be based from the absolute beginning of the clip (:07 means 7 seconds into the clip, 1:09 means 1 minute and 9 seconds into the clip, etc.). The expected content would be jotted into the space to the right of the time indicator so that it can be screened prior to the activation of the key layer.

With the widespread use of nonlinear editing systems, it is not uncommon to find video clips with all of the character generation pre-edited. If this protocol is in place at a given news operation, the job (and stress level) of the Director, the AD, the Graphics operator, and the Technical Director (TD) can be greatly reduced.

Variations

Another technique to convey clip information is to locate it more readily and target it to members of the production staff that require it. For example, the duration of a clip, information most needed by the Director and AD, might be located in the left-hand column of the script. Graphic requirements could be handled with a separate form that originates with the producing staff, the editing staff, or both. An expanded rundown could also be used for some of the necessary information regarding any given clip. The concept to remember is that key information regarding the tape clip must be conveyed in some manner to the production staff that requires it.

Assistant Directing and Directing

Assistant Directing

The responsibility for managing the technical requirements of a live television newscast falls primarily to the Director. A large part of the job of directing is "knowing what to say and when to say it." Therefore, the Assistant Director's (AD) contribution to the process really is significant in terms of figuring out "when to say it."

Show time

The AD (or Production Assistant) is responsible for timing the show— forward and backward. The AD must be able to announce, at any given moment, how much time has elapsed into the show, as well as how much time remains. For example, the AD might announce, "We are 10 minutes 10 seconds into the show, and we have 19 minutes 50 seconds remaining."

In order to control and calculate show time, the AD will refer to two clocks (usually located prominently in the control room). One is a clock that shows real time (the time of day) and is typically calibrated via satellite or by using the Internet. Real time is exact. The network and the local station are often coordinated to the tenth of a second.

The other clock is a large-format counter that will be activated at the very beginning of the newscast. The counter will either count up from zero or be preset with a duration (28:30 is a common example) and begin to count down when activated. Thus, everyone who can see either clock can coordinate with the AD in terms of the timing of the entire program.

If the show is running short (not enough material), segments can be added or extended (ever wonder why the weather segment and sportscast vary so much in length?). If the show is running long (too much material or a lot of breaking news has been added), segments can be deleted ("killed") or shortened (like the 45-second weather forecast). The show must end precisely so that the station can remain aligned with feeds from the network. (NBC's Brian Williams is not going to wait for a station in Dallas to "finish" the local newscast.)

Backtiming

The task of backtiming and forward timing a television program is the responsibility of an Assistant Director (or Production Assistant). In the absence of an AD, it is common for the newscast Producer to handle show timing.

Timing the program is usually handled with a simple digital clock. Either one starts the clock from zero and allows it to count up, or one sets the expected duration of the show on the clock and allows it to count down.

In either case, the AD should be able to tell how much time has elapsed and how much time is left at-a-glance.

Pre-recorded video clips need to be timed as well. The duration of the clip is the first concern.

In the VO/SOT type of clip, a second concern is the precise moment the SOT portion will commence. Audio will need to track the audio from the tape at this exact moment; and, the anchor will need to be finished speaking.

Finally, the third matter of timing a clip concerns the windows of time when CG can be keyed over the tape (for name, location, or other information).

To handle these three timing tasks, it is common for Assistant Directors to use an analog stopwatch (like the *60 Minutes* watch) that features a sweeping second hand. The first task is handled by a process of visual math. The latter two concerns can be handled by merely reading the watch as it counts up from zero.

Visual math is a procedure by which, at-a-glance, the AD can subtract the amount of time elapsed in a tape clip — from the known total running time of the tape clip — with the result of the time remaining in the clip.

To begin the process, the AD makes a mental note of the total running time of the clip. If the clip is 1:23, the AD visually imprints a line across the watch face that crosses through the 23-second mark.

Next the AD visually imprints a perpendicular line to the first (see page 152) with the result of a cross.

Each quarter of the watch face represents 15 seconds.

When the watch is started from zero, the second hand will begin sweeping toward the first line. When it arrives, 1:15 seconds is left in the tape clip.

When the second hand reaches the second line, 1 minute is left in the tape clip.

When the second hand reaches the third line, 45 seconds is left in the tape clip (and so on).

Timing Video Clips

The other timing task the AD will typically contend with concerns the video clips. Each clip needs to be timed. The Director (and everyone else) needs to know exactly when a clip is ending so that a transition to the next audio and video source may be made smoothly.

The timing information on the clip can be communicated to the AD in any number of ways (on the script, on a font sheet, in a column on the rundown). As soon as a clip begins, the AD will normally activate a stopwatch.

By subtracting the stopwatch indication from the clip time, the AD knows "how much time is left" in the tape. Believe it or not, this "backtiming" task is fairly difficult. Doing math on the fly in this manner is rarely simple. For example, take a normal digital stopwatch and start it from zero. Now, imagine you are timing a clip of 1:23 (1 minute, 23 seconds in length). Glance at the watch, do the math, and convey the result (out loud). By the time most folks say it, the information is incorrect.

Programmable counters can be used if the time gap between clips is great enough to permit the AD to program in the next clip length and activate a countdown. However, in many news environments, this is not the case. To get around this problem, many ADs continue to utilize analog stopwatches to work out the timing of video clips. To "do the math" with an analog watch is much easier as the calculation is partially visual.

We don't need an AD

It is important to point out that in most small- and in some medium-market television news operations, the responsibility for all timing tasks falls to a Newscast Producer or the Director. Or, the News Producer will handle show timing and the Director will handle clip timing. Simply put, the AD job does not exist as a separate crew position at many small- and medium-market stations.

The AD Will ImagineThis Line Across the Watch Face First.

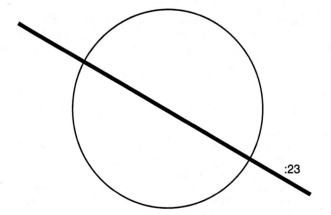

:23

VO/SOT

Not only is the AD concerned with the length of each clip, but also he or she must account for clips that may be broken into VO portions that are edited to SOT portions. The transition point between the VO portion and the SOT portion is mission critical for the production person assigned to Audio. It is at this point that the anchor's mic will be cut and the audio from a video tape recorder (VTR) brought in "full." At this point, the anchor must have completed the prepared script (or be skilled enough to ad lib into the bite) as well.

In order for the anchor to do this, the Floor Director will count him or her into the bite (the SOT portion) by relaying the count from the AD. Thus, it will go something like this: Assume the VO/SOT is 30 seconds long. The VO portion is :25 and the SOT that follows is :05. When the Director rolls the tape, the AD will begin the stopwatch.

When the watch shows :15, there are 10 seconds left to the bite. The AD will say, "Count in 10, 9, 8, 7, 6, 5, 4, 3, 2, 1." The Floor Director will be relaying these commands to the anchor (using hand signals) as the anchor finishes the prepared script. The anchor must be finished in time (often the anchor has to speed up) or the microphone may be "upcut" as the Audio operator crosscuts to the VTR audio source.

A common variation on the counting process is to count the anchor directly through the use of IFB (switched talkback).

The AD Will Imagine This Line Across the Watch Face Second.

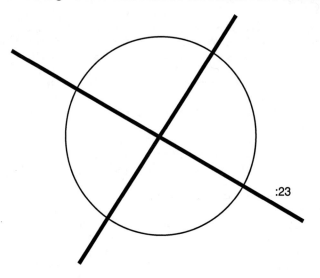

:23

SOT/VO

Not only is the point of transition important from VO to SOT, the reverse is also true. When an SOT cuts to a VO, the Audio operator will need to open the anchor's microphone and "cut" the VTR source audio—exactly as it ends. Although the process does not involve the Floor Director "counting" with the talent, he or she will need to cue the talent to provide the voice-over for that portion of the tape.

A common variant that avoids the VO/SOT timing difficulty is only slightly smoother for the production crew. Separating the VO portion and the SOT portion onto separate tapes (rolled from separate VTRs) can be a work-around. The SOT merely needs to be rolled in such a way as to "hit" the program precisely as the anchor is finishing the VO portion.

While there is no danger of upcutting the anchor or missing any audio from the bite, the crew is running the risk of tape failure. The danger is that the SOT will not (or cannot) roll for some reason, and the anchor is left to look foolish for introducing a bite that will not be viewed. However, if the producing staff avoids "previewing" the SOT in the VO—avoids "We ran into Coach Medoff after the game and here is what he had to say"—the VO will merely stand alone. The Director (and crew) can simply continue to the next story in the event of tape failure. The advantages to separating the VO from the SOT really bear on the AD, the Floor Director, the anchor, and Audio. The disadvantages affect the Director, the Technical Director (TD), and Tape. A zero sum game, perhaps.

Character generation

Another timing task that involves the video clip concerns the point at which character generation may be required to be keyed (or layered) over the video clip. The AD may use the same stopwatch used for clip time for this task or may use an additional watch (digital or analog).

The point at which a particular graphic is to be brought up is usually very tight (often a window of no longer than 5 seconds). The graphic might be a location, like "Portales, New Mexico," or a name, like "Dale Hoskins, UFO Witness." Names tend to be much more time critical as the person may only appear during a short sound bite.

The AD, then, will need to be ready to call the command to "key" in the graphic. Again, the timing of graphics is often delegated to another crew member (some directors also act as their own ADs due to common "control" issues among the group). Yet, it is not uncommon for the TD or Graphics operator to handle the task. And, with the widespread use of nonlinear editing systems, character generation is commonly pre-produced (edited) on the tape prior to air.

Visual Math

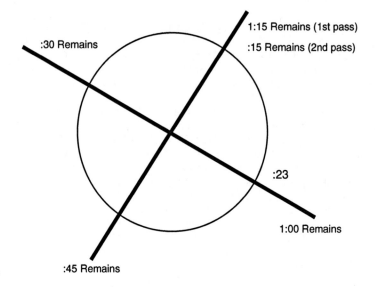

1:15 Remains (1st pass)

:15 Remains (2nd pass)

:30 Remains

:23

1:00 Remains

:45 Remains

Directing

Introduction

The job of the Director is to "drive the bus." All of the other crew positions are coordinated by the command cues the Director gives as the show commences. To know "what to say and when to say it," the Director will primarily rely on the script, the rundown, and the critical timing information regarding any roll-ins (video clips).

The language the Director uses when giving these command cues is like a shorthand. It allows one person to communicate with the entire crew in an efficient manner. Learning the language is easy. Performing the language live is something else entirely.

No matter how well written the news program may be, no matter how skilled and experienced the producing staff and anchors, the show will fail if the Director cannot coordinate the production effort.

Director Wayne Nesbitt has said, "Directing is like running in front of a train. Either you are leading the train down the tracks, or being run over." In live television, there is no "time out" beyond that which is built into the show (commercial breaks).

The command cue language

The command language must be straightforward. A Director should give commands in a two-step flow: a "ready cue" followed by a "do it" cue. For example, a Director might say, "Ready Camera One" followed by "Take Camera One."

However, the process gains complexity as audio information is added. For example, a Director might say, "Ready Camera One with a mic and a cue" followed by "Take Camera One, mic, and cue."

Information can be added or deleted to the command syntax as necessary. For example, the mic number can be added and the word "camera" deleted. "Ready One with Mic 4 and a cue" followed by "Take One, mic, and cue."

A Director's particular style will determine the command syntax, but it is easy to see how giving the mic number might get muddled with the camera number in the mix of the headset chatter.

Another protocol you may already have noticed is to always follow the video cue with the audio cue. "Ready Camera Two with a mic and cue." Remember the basic form—a "ready" cue followed by a "do it" cue. It is the only way the crew can respond to direction calmly. Imagine a Director who never gives "ready" cues.

Command Cue Lexicon

Aside
Bust
Center-Up (Camera)
Clear
Come-Up (TD)
Crab (Camera)
Crash (Camera)
Cross-Fade (Audio)
Cue (Floor Director)
Cut (TD)
Dead
Dissolve (TD)
Dolly (Camera)
Downstream (TD)
Fade (Audio)
Fade (TD)
Fade to Black (TD and Audio)
Fade Up (TD)
Font (TD)
Full Track (Audio)
Go (Audio)
Loosen (Camera)
Lose (TD)
Mic (Audio)
Mix (TD)
Pan (Camera)
Pedestal (Camera)
Pull (TD)
Push (TD)
Re-Rack (Tape)
Ready
Roll (Tape)
Roll Record (Tape)
Set Focus (Camera)
Sneak (Audio)
Spin (Graphics)
Stand By
Swing (Floor Director)
Take (TD)
Tighten (Camera)
Tilt (Camera)
Track (Audio)
Track (Camera)
Truck (Camera)
Wipe (TD)
Zoom (Camera)

Cameras Versus VTRs

In order to differentiate and separate camera commands from tape commands, the most common protocol in news is to number cameras and to letter VTRs.

Savvy directors will continue the separation in the command syntax by "readying" cameras and using "stand by" for VTRs. For example, "Stand by Tape A" and "Roll Tape A ... take it" versus "Ready Camera One" and "Take One."

Add the audio information to the VTR command, and the command might say, "Stand by Tape A, full track is coming on A, roll Tape A, track, and take it," or "Stand by Tape B, NAT on Channel 2, roll Tape B, take it, sneak NAT (or 'track NAT')."

Remember, information can be added to and deleted from the command syntax as necessary—and it is only really necessary to identify the VTR once. For example, "Stand by Tape A, full track" followed by "Roll, track, take."

Other commands and many variations exist in the command cue lexicon. The command to activate a key might take any one of the following forms: "Stand by downstream" followed by "Downstream" followed by "Ready to lose downstream" followed by "Lose," or "Ready to font" followed by "Font" followed by "Ready to lose" followed by "Lose."

See the command cue lexicon (and some variants) in the figure on page 156. As a beginning Director, it is valuable to spend some time listening and watching "Director's cuts" of newscasts. The audio mix includes the headset chatter with the program video so that you can see (and hear) the connection between the command cue and the result.

Who does what?

Part I

Figuring out the command cues can take time for the production crew. Consider how many people are affected by the following command, "Stand by Tape A, full track is coming on A, roll Tape A, track, and take."

On "Stand by Tape A," the Tape Operator has loaded the correct tape and cued to the correct video clip in VTR A. The clip is cued (on pause) inside of a countdown at three and the Operator is poised to press play.

The TD has selected VTR A in the preview bus.

On "full track is coming on A," the Audio Operator prepares to cross-fade to the two audio channels that will be fed from VTR A.

On "roll tape A," the Tape Operator presses play.

On "track," the Audio Operator will cross-fade to the VTR audio.

On "take," the TD will transition to VTR A as the active program source.

Part II

Or, consider the following command, "Ready Camera One with a mic and a cue, take, mic, and cue."

On "Ready Camera One," the TD (VM) selects Camera One to the preview bus.

The Camera One Operator is poised with the appropriate shot.

The Floor Director is standing next to Camera One and is at Stand by (arm up, palm out, fingers up).

On "take," the TD transitions to Camera One as the active program source.

On "mic," the Audio Operator will "bring up" the appropriate anchor microphone as the program audio source.

On "cue," the Floor Director will cue the anchor in the studio to begin (swinging the arm downward). All of this illustrates that when a Director gives a command, a lot of crew members can be responding almost at the same time.

Marking a Script

One of the procedures the Director will follow involves "marking" the script with reminders (memory jogs) as to what command needs to be said. Although every Director marks a script differently, a common syntax is useful to learn the marking process.

"OC" stands for on camera. A Director may jot OC1 to indicate that a particular segment is to be handled by Camera One. OC2 would indicate that the primary video would be from Camera Two—and so on.

The mark for a tape clip is a bit more complex. First, a **roll cue** must be located and marked in the script. A roll cue is a word that the anchor is to say in the few moments before a clip will be rolled and activated to program. Depending on the average speed of the anchor's speech, the roll cue could be an entire sentence or so "back" from the point of the tape hit.

Once the roll cue is located and "marked" (some directors will circle it), the VTR information will need to be marked on the script. One technique is to make a roll box. In the example, notice the word "roll" and the box below it. The word "roll" is a memory jog aimed at the roll command. The VTR letter can be marked in the box—in this example it is VTR A. Finally, an arrow can be drawn from the roll box toward the roll cue in order to direct the eye.

Thus, while the anchor is reading the introductory portion of the story to Camera One (as indicated by the OC1 mark), the Director can give the ready cue for VTR A. When the Director hears the anchor hit the roll cue, he or she can "roll" the tape and "take" it as the program source as the anchor finishes the story introduction.

Other common marks include "FTB" for fade to black, "MC" for Master Control, "###" for the end of a segment (an old throwback—ask your journalism professor), and "CD" for—you guessed it—compact disc.

An Example of a Marked Script Page for a Reader

140 – METEOR SHOWER
ANCHOR 1

OC1

Oc1

STAR-GAZERS... GET READY.
ASTRONOMERS SAY TONIGHT'S
METEOR SHOWER MAY BE THE
MOST IMPRESSIVE IN DECADES.
RESIDENTS OF THE MIDWEST GOT
AN EARLY VIEW OF THE LEONID
METEOR SHOWER—AND MANY
OF THEM CALLED AUTHORITIES
TO REPORT U-F-OS. THE
METEORS ARE DUST AND ICE
PELLETS FROM THE COMET
TEMPEL-TUTTLE. ASTRONOMERS
SAY YOU COULD SEE AS MANY
AS FIVE-THOUSAND PER HOUR.
THEY SAY THE BEST TIME TO
WATCH THE LEONID SHOWER IS
IN THE EARLY MORNING HOURS.
THE PEAK IS SUPPOSED TO BE
JUST AFTER DARK... BUT LAST
YEAR IN WILLIMANTIC... IT WAS
OFF BY A FEW HOURS. SOURCES
FROM LOWELL OBSERVATORY
TELL US THAT THE BEST WAY TO
SEE THE METEOR SHOWER IS JUST
TO LOOK AT THE SKY... AND THE
DARKER THE AREA YOU ARE IN...
THE BETTER. ###

###

Practice

It is important that new directors do not attempt to write out, verbatim, the command cues needed for a program on the script. The television program is in the monitors, not the script. If you are reading commands, you are not directing. The script is only one tool in the procedure of directing, and you must learn to merely glance at it as the show progresses. By all means, one should practice command cues in whatever fashion seems to work well for the individual. However, it is good form to always direct from marks so that the new Director does not come to awkwardly rely on a script of command cues.

The time period immediately prior to the newscast is a busy one. Final preparations are made that concern both the producing staff and production crew. In the final minutes, Master Control will confirm communication with the control room as well as monitor the incoming flow of audio and video from any remote units (microwave or satellite). The crew member at Audio and the Technical Director will reconfirm all audio and video sourcing. At the appointed time, Master Control will count the studio into the show by counting down the minutes and seconds and finish by activating the studio as the master source for the station—the studio is now "up." It is at this point that the program is in the hands of the production crew as the Director "calls" the show.

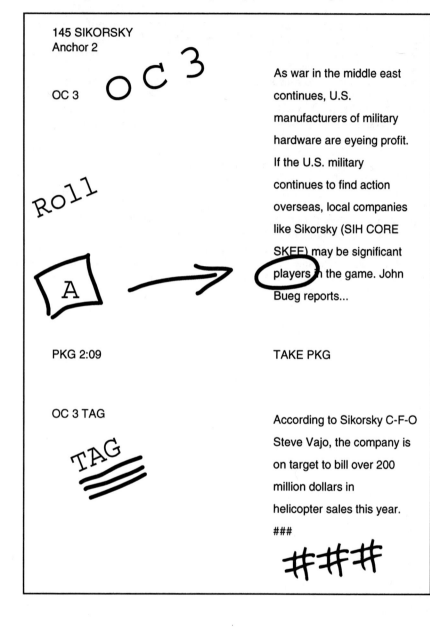

145 SIKORSKY
Anchor 2

OC 3

As war in the middle east
continues, U.S.
manufacturers of military
hardware are eyeing profit.
If the U.S. military
continues to find action
overseas, local companies
like Sikorsky (SIH CORE
SKEE) may be significant
players in the game. John
Bueg reports...

PKG 2:09

TAKE PKG

OC 3 TAG

According to Sikorsky C-F-O
Steve Vajo, the company is
on target to bill over 200
million dollars in
helicopter sales this year.
###

Glossary

A2:   Audio Assistant.

AP: Associate Producer.

Affiliate: (see Network Affiliate)

Air Check: a master recording of a television show.

Anchors (see Talent)

Aside: a command cue that temporarily suspends a segment from the rundown.

Aspect Ratio: the ratio of width to height of the video image. SDTV is 4:3. Wide-screen video is 16:9.

Assistant Director (AD) or Production Assistant (PA):   production crew member responsible for timing a television program.

Atmosphere (see Natural Sound):   UK.

Audio Operator: production crew member responsible for operating the audio board.

Audio Board: controls the selection, flow, modification, and mix of audio sources. An audio selection device. The final output is Audio Program.

Audio Console (see Audio Board)

Audio Monitor: a speaker in the control room used to monitor Audio Program.

Audio Program: the final mix of audio sent out for recording or broadcast.

Audio Snake: a cable containing bundled audio lines that terminates in a box containing multiple audio hookups.

Backlight: a lighting instrument located 45 degrees up and to the rear of a talent position. A backlight provides visual separation of the talent from the background.

Backfocus (or Flangeback):   the focus adjustment between the camera imaging device (CCD) and the lens.

Barndoor: a four-flap sheet metal lighting accessory mounted to the front of a lighting instrument that permits greater control in how a light is aimed.

Battens (or Barrels):   the lighting grid is made up of pipes called battens. Lighting instruments are mounted to battens.

Beltpack: a small box that is a component of the intercom system. The box connects the headset and audio cable, and controls intercom channel selection, headset volume, and headset mic activation.

Biscuit (see Tripod Shoe)

Blacked: a tape with control track or time code pre-recorded.

Block: a section of a television program that occurs between commercial breaks. A half-hour news program is often broken into four blocks.

BNC: a type of professional grade, locking video connector.

Broad: a non-focusing flood light shaped like a small box.

Broadcast Engineer: production crew member and station employee responsible for audio and video routing, signal quality, signal balance, and equipment repair.

Bug: a small graphic (usually a logo) keyed onto Video Program signal at Master Control.

Bugged: describes any video containing a bug.

Bump: a transitional video clip that is played at the end of a program block just prior to commercial break. Often, the bump is used to tease content coming up later in the program.

Bust: a command cue to stop recording the television program.

Camera (see Studio Television Camera)

Camera Cable: a cable that carries the video from the studio television camera to the control room.

Camera Control Unit (CCU): a remote control for the studio television camera that is located in the control room. The CCU controls power, color balance, iris, and white and black balance.

Camera Operator: production crew member responsible for operating the studio television camera.

Camera Plate: a flat metal plate used in conjunction with a tripod shoe to attach a camera unit to a tripod or pedestal head.

Caption Generator (CapGen) (see Character Generator): UK.

Channel One: a channel of audio sourced from a video clip.

Channel Two (see Channel One)

Character Generator (CG) or Caption Generator (CapGen): a computer located in the control room that generates video text (words) that can be keyed over a picture or used alone as a video source.

Charge-Coupled Device (CCD): the imaging device inside the studio television camera. A CCD (or chip) converts light into a video signal. Professional cameras have three CCDs, one each to image red, green, and blue. The larger the CCD, the higher the possible resolution. Professional-grade CCDs are a half inch or larger.

Chroma Key Wall: a set piece that is painted a green or blue color (or a cyc or curtain that is dyed similarly). When viewed through the studio camera, the color can be isolated, removed, and replaced in the chroma key process. The weather forecast is usually delivered from the chroma key wall.

Chrominance: color saturation.

Clear: a command cue that indicates that audio from the VTRs, microphones, or cameras is no longer active to program.

Clip: adjusts the relative strength of the video layer in the keying process. Clip adjustment is located on the video switcher.

Clip Sheet (see Font Sheet): UK.

Clip Time or Duration: the precise length of a video clip.

Color Bars: a video test pattern that contains colored bars.

Column Lock: a pedestal lock that prevents the camera from moving vertically.

Come Up: a command cue that instructs the TD to engage a dissolve (or fade) from black to the video source in preview.

Command Cue Language: the shorthand language that permits the Director to speak to and instruct the entire production crew at once.

Control Room or Gallery: a physical space containing the staff and equipment that controls the flow and selection of audio and video in a television program.

Crab (see Truck): UK.

164

Crash: a command cue (UK) indicating that the Camera Operator may move, reposition, or reframe the studio camera as quickly (and roughly) as needed.

Cross-fade: a command cue for Audio to bring one audio source down while at the same time bringing another audio source up.

Cue: a command given by the Director to the production staff to begin a task or procedure. A command given to the talent to begin speaking. A video clip is cued when it is ready to be activated.

Cut: an instant transition between two video sources.

Cut Number: when multiple video clips are located on an individual tape, the cut number refers to the clip position on the tape.

Cut Sheet (see Font Sheet)

Cyc light: a cyc light is a flood light designed to illuminate the cyc (see below). Cyc lights will either be mounted on the ground and aimed upward or grid mounted and aimed downward. Cyc lights are commonly colored using gels.

Cyclorama (Cyc): a curtain or flat fabric panel that is available as a backdrop in the studio. Usually, cycs help to absorb echo and are non-reflective.

Dead: a segment that has been permanently discarded.

Decibel (dB): a scale for measuring the strength of an audio signal.

Digital Video Effects (DVE): a special effects processor hooked into the video switcher. A video source can be routed to the DVE, modified, and looped back to the switcher as a new source.

Director: leader and supervisor of the production staff. Responsible for using the command cue language to "call" a television program.

Dissolve: a video transition where one video source is gradually replaced by another.

Dolly (see Pedestal)

Dolly or Track: a command cue for the Camera Operator to roll the entire camera unit toward or away from the set.

Dolly Operator (see Grip): UK.

Downstream Key (DSK): a key that is electronically processed in the switcher after all transition and effects have been added to program video.

Drag (see Friction)

Duration (see Clip Time): UK.

Duratran a backlit, translucent image embedded in the flat wall of a set.

Electronic Still-Store (ESS): a graphics computer (or function of a graphics computer) that captures, stores, manages, sequences, and displays still images.

Ellipsoidal: a type of spot light used to create distinct shapes, patterns, and art on a set. An effects light.

Engineer (see Broadcast Engineer)

Engineering: a physical place in a television station where equipment is repaired (called the bench) or the engineering staff is located.

Equalization: the process of increasing or decreasing the sensitivity of a specific audio frequency or group of frequencies.

Fade (audio related): to slowly increase or decrease the strength of an audio source.

Fade (video related): to engage a dissolve (mix) either up from black to an active video source or down to black (fade to black).

Faders: control the input and output flow of audio through the audio board.

Fader Bar or Paddle: a T-shaped handle in the transition area on the video switcher that permits manual control of wipes and dissolves.

Feature (see Package)

Fill Light: the second light of the three-point lighting strategy. Located 45 degrees up and to the right of the talent position, the fill light may be a spot light or a flood light.

Filtering: a function of the audio board that permits the isolation of a specific frequency and the removal of all frequency response above or below that point.

Flats: vertical set pieces used to create background walls for a set.

Flood Lights: lighting instruments that generate a type of light ray that is nonparallel and distanced apart. The quality of light is soft or diffuse and the beam spread is wide.

Floor Director or Floor Manager: production crew member responsible for managing and communicating with the talent. Floor Directors cue the talent, relay commands and timing information from the control room, assist other studio crew members, and are responsible for studio safety.

Floor Manager (see Floor Director): UK.

Focus: the property of visual clarity established between the camera lens and the targeted object.

Font Sheet or Clip Sheet: a document that contains information regarding a video clip (duration, audio characteristics, story type, graphics requirements).

Footcandle (FC): a measure of light based on the amount of luminance given by a single candle at a distance of 12 inches.

Framing: the composition of a camera shot refers to framing.

Freeze: refers to the capture of one frame of video to use in an ESS (electronic still-store).

Fresnel: a focusing spot lighting instrument used for lighting people and set materials.

Friction or Drag: an adjustment on the pedestal head that increases or decreases the relative resistance for the tilt control (tilt friction) or the pan control (pan friction).

FTB: shorthand for fade to black.

FX: shorthand for effects (usually graphics or DVE).

Gaffers: production crew member responsible for hanging, aiming, and tuning the lighting instruments. Gaffers are often electricians.

Gain (audio related): a control on the audio board that permits the amplification of an incoming signal.

Gain (key related): a control on the video switcher that permits the amplification of the video source assigned to the key bus.

Gain (video related): amplification of a video signal.

166

Gallery (see Control Room): UK.

Gel: a colored sheet of non-flammable plastic used to color the light output of a lighting instrument.

Go: command cue (UK) for audio to activate an audio source.

Gobo: a logo or pattern cut from metal that can be inserted in front of an ellipsoidal light. The logo or pattern will project onto the surface the light is aimed toward.

Graphics: production crew member responsible for creating, managing, sequencing, and playing back character generation, still images, 3D models, and animations.

Graphics Computer: a computer designated for the creation of character generation, still images, 3D models, and animations.

Grips or Dolly Operators: production crew members responsible for assembling sets, managing boom-mounted microphones, managing jib-mounted cameras, and other manual tasks.

Ground Row: a lighting instrument that contains multiple in-line lamps used to wash light upward.

HDTV: high-definition television: any television signal that contains 720 or greater lines of resolution.

Headroom: the visual space between the top of the talent's head and the top of the image frame.

Headset: a component of the intercom unit worn on the head containing a headphone and a microphone.

Ingest: the process of loading video into a video server. If the video is analog, the process involves digitization.

Intercom Unit: the off-air communication system utilized by the staff of the control room, the studio, Master Control, and other production crew as needed.

Input Fader: a sliding knob on the audio board that controls the input signal strength of an individual audio source.

Instant Start: a type of VTR that permits the videotape to attain operating speed without a ppre-roll.

Interrupt Foldback (IFB) or Switched Talkback: an audio feed of the entire program mix (excluding the anchor's own microphone) from the audio board to a small earphone worn by the talent on the set. IFB allows the talent to monitor Audio Program, and it also permits the producing staff to cut into the feed and speak directly to the anchor.

Item (see Slug): UK.

Jackfield (see Patch Panel)

Jib: a camera mounted to the end of a long, metal arm.

Key: a video layer.

Key Bus: a row of buttons on the video switcher that permits the direct selection of the key video source.

Key Light: the first light of the three-point lighting strategy. Located 45 degrees up and to the left of the talent position, the key light is usually a spot light.

Key Shot: a shot that includes an over-the-shoulder graphic with the anchor.

Kicker: a light aimed at the background of a set from a left or right position off screen.

Lavaliere: the most common type of studio microphone. Also known as a lapel mic, the unit is small and unobtrusive.

Lead-In: a short introductory sentence given on camera by an anchor to introduce a video clip or live shot.

Leadroom or Looking Room: visual space given in the frame for the talent to walk into or look into.

Light Meter: a handheld meter that measures the intensity or amount of light.

Lighting Board: a console that controls power flow to each lighting instrument. Permits dimming, grouping, and fading of the lighting instruments.

Lighting Grid: the large network of pipes and electrical service located in the ceiling of the studio.

Lighting Instrument: a generic term for any light used in the studio.

Line Source an audio source that is generated at a normal signal strength (for example, CD players, VTRs).

Linear Editing: tape-to-tape, chronological editing. May be digital or analog.

Live Inject (see Live Shot): UK.

Live Shot or Live Inject: a story format that features a reporter who is live on the scene. A live shot can be returned to the station via microwave, satellite, telephone, or the Internet.

Live to Tape: conducting a television program from beginning to end as if the program is a live broadcast.

Location (L): the physical location of a video clip. Refers to a specific VTR, server, or computer file.

Locked: a command cue that indicates a VTR is operating at speed and in the expected mode.

Looking Room (see Leadroom): UK.

Loosen a command cue for the television camera operator to zoom out.

Lose: a command cue for the Technical Director to deactivate a key.

Luminance brightness.

Master Control or Transmission Control: a physical space in the television station where the output of the station is controlled from. Incoming microwave and satellite feeds are received and managed from Master Control. Commercial breaks, network feeds, pre-recorded programming, and live studio programming are controlled from this location.

Master Fader: a fader on the audio board that controls the signal strength of Audio Program.

Master Lock: a large, spring-loaded pin located through the pedestal head. A master lock prevents the camera from tilting.

Mic Source audio generated from a microphone is weaker than audio generated by a line source by as much as 50 dB. Mic sources need to be amplified before mixing with line sources.

Microphone (Mic):   a transducer. A microphone changes sound waves to an electromagnetic signal.

Midstream Key: a key that is electronically processed in the switcher at the same time that the transition effects are added to program video.

Mix (see Dissolve)

Mix Effects Bus (M/E):   a group of three rows of buttons on a video switcher. An ME is made up of a preview bus (bottom row), a program bus (middle row), and a key bus (top row).

Mix Minus or Program Clean Feed (PCF):   Audio Program with the source audio from the anchor microphone removed. Permits the anchor to hear the show without danger of creating a feedback loop or distraction by a delayed feedback of the anchor's own audio.

Monitor (see Video Monitor or Audio Monitor)

Monitor Wall: feature of the control room containing numerous video monitors that reveal video sources that can be selected from preview video and program video.

Mono one unique, individual channel of audio.

Natural Sound (NAT) or Atmosphere (ATMOS):   audio from a video clip that is without reporter narration. Natural sound is "location" sound, such as birds chirping, wind noise, waves crashing, glass breaking, gunfire, or explosions.

Network Affiliate: a television station that is formally associated with a network. The relationship permits the local station to use the resources of the network (content, satellite time, etc.) and the network to "reach" a large audience.

News Desk: a prominent feature of the news set where the anchors sit and deliver the newscast.

News Director: the ultimate producer responsible for a television news operation.

Nonlinear Editing (NLE):   computer-based, non-chronological editing. Common software includes Apple Computer's Final Cut Pro, Adobe Premiere, and AVID.

NTSC (see SDTV):   National Television Standards Council.

On Camera (OC):   a story format where the anchor merely reads a story to a camera with no associated video clip.

Outcue or Outwords (see Standard Outcue):   the last thing seen or heard on a video clip.

Output Fader: a sliding knob on the audio board that controls the output signal strength of Audio Program.

Outwords (see Outcue) UK.

Overmodulation: an audio signal that is too strong. The electrical strength will distort the signal.

Over-the-Shoulder (OTS):   a camera shot of one person from a position behind a second person, revealing the back of the head and shoulders of the second person (UK). OTS is sometimes used to refer to a key shot (USA).

Package (PKG):   a story format that features an on-camera introduction by the news anchor followed by a pre-recorded video clip.

Pad: extra material edited to or remaining on the tail of a video clip.

Paddle (see Fader Bar): UK.

Pan: a command cue for the Camera Operator to pivot the camera to the left or to the right.

Pan Lock: a pedestal lock that prevents the camera from pivoting left and right.

PAR: Parabolic Aluminum Reflector Light: a type of lighting instrument with a fixed beam spread.

Patch Panel: an input/output box of audio, video, intercom, and clock connections located on a studio wall.

Pedestal: the mount for the studio television camera.

Pedestal: a command cue for the Camera Operator to raise or lower the height of the camera.

Pedestal Steering Wheel: a wheel located mid-level on a studio camera pedestal that is used for pushing, pulling, and steering a studio television camera.

Percent of Modulation (PM): a measurement of audio signal strength on a 0 to 100 scale.

Phantom Power: a feature of some audio boards that sends a 48-volt channel of direct current (DC) upstream in order to power a studio microphone.

Post-Fade: an audio source after modulation by the audio board fader strip.

Post-Production: the process of or facility for video editing.

Pre-Fade: an audio source prior to modulation by the audio board fader strip.

Pre-Roll: rewinding and pausing a video tape 3 or more seconds before the beginning of a video clip. Engaging "Play" on a VTR that is pre-rolled permits the VTR to attain operating speed prior to the beginning of the clip.

Presenters (see Talent): UK.

Preview: the video source that is on deck, or next in line.

Preview Bus: a row of buttons on the video switcher that permits the direct selection of the preview video source.

Preview Monitor: a monitor that reveals the preview video source.

Producer: the writer or a member of the writing staff.

Production Assistant (see Assistant Director): UK.

Program: the final mix of audio and/or video sources that is assembled as a television program.

Program Bus: a row of buttons on the video switcher that permits the direct selection of the program video source.

Program Clean Feed (see Mix Minus): UK.

RCA: a non-locking, consumer-grade video and audio connector.

Re-Rack: a command cue for the tape operator to reload and cue video clips.

Reader (see On Camera)

Ready (see also Stand By): a command cue to prepare for a task that follows.

Risers: platforms used in set construction to raise the actual and visual height of a set.

Roll: a command cue for Tape to play a video clip.

Roll Cue: a specific word in the script identified by the Director as the cue to convey a roll command. Usually a roll cue is selected 3 seconds prior to the expected take point of the clip.

Roll-Record: a command cue for Tape to engage a VTR to record the program.

Routing Switcher: a device that directs incoming audio or video signals to specific destinations.

Run Number: an identifying number assigned to a specific, individual segment in a television program.

Rundown or Running Order: an outline of a television program that lists the segments of the program.

Running Order (see Rundown): UK.

Scene Dock: a room (often adjacent to the studio) used for the storage of set materials.

Scoop: a type of flood light shaped like a large mixing bowl.

SDTV (see NTSC) standard-definition television: any television signal made up of 525 lines of resolution at 30 frames per second.

Segment Number (see Run Number)

Shot Sheet: a list of camera shots that includes framing and composition information.

Show Time: the total duration of a television program.

Signal Strength: a measure of electrical strength of a video or audio signal.

Sky Cyc: a flood light mounted in the grid (often a softbox) that is purposed to wash the cyc with light from the top downward.

Slug or Item: a short nickname given to a segment of a television program.

Snake (see Audio Snake)

Sneak: a command cue to slowly fade in an audio source.

Softlight (Softbox) a box shaped flood light.

Solo: a switch on the audio board that permits the operator to isolate and monitor a single audio source apart from the mix.

Sound on Tape (SOT): indicates that source audio is contained on both channels of a video clip.

Spill: unwanted light. Light that has "spilled" over the intended target.

Spin: a command cue for graphics to activate a sequence of graphics pages or animation.

Spot Lights: lighting instruments that generate a type of light ray that is parallel and close together. The quality of light is hard and the beam spread is tight.

Stand By (see also Ready): a command cue to prepare for a task that follows.

Standard Outcue: refers to the standard manner of ending a taped segment by a reporter. Usually, this is the name of the reporter followed by the name of the news organization: "I'm Todd Hicks, Laramie News 9."

Stereo: two unique, individual, separate channels of audio.

Studio: the large space in a television station where the set for a television program is located. The studio contains lighting equipment, audio acquisition equipment, and the studio television cameras.

Studio Television Camera: a device that creates a video signal from reflected light.

Swing: a command cue to motion the talent from one camera to another.

Switched Talkback (see Interrupt Foldback): UK.

T-Bar (see Fader Bar)

Tag: the anchor's on-camera closing comment following a taped segment.

Take: a command cue to "cut" the video source from preview to program.

Talent: generic term for the individuals who host television programs.

Tally Light: located on the viewfinder, the tally light indicates whether the camera is "active" or selected to the program bus.

Tape: production crew member responsible for the management and playback of video clips in a television program. Tape is often responsible for recording the program as well.

Tape Number: an identifying number assigned to a physical videotape.

Technical Director (TD) or Vision Mixer (VM): production crew member responsible for operating the video switcher.

Teleprompter: production crew member responsible for the management, recall, and display of the prompting script.

Teleprompting Computer: a computer located in the control room that contains the script for the television program. The teleprompting software converts the script from text to video and allows the controller to "scroll" through the script.

Three-Point Lighting: a lighting strategy that uses three lighting instruments per talent position. The lights are the key light, the fill light, and the back light.

Tight Out: a video clip that ends immediately after the outcue. A video clip with no pad.

Tighten: a command cue for the camera to zoom in, tightening the framing.

Tilt: a command cue for the studio Camera Operator to either pivot the camera upward or downward.

Tilt Lock: a pedestal lock that prevents the camera from tilting up or tilting down.

Tone: a 1-kHZ audio signal used to calibrate the audio board and the VTRs.

Total Running Time (TRT): refers to the complete duration of a television program or video clip.

Track: a command cue for audio to fade in the audio source from a video clip.

Tracking (see Dolly): UK.

Transmission Control (see Master Control): UK.

Trim (see Gain—audio related)

Tripod Shoe: a small plate used to attach the camera plate to the tripod.

Truck or Crab: a command cue for the studio Camera Operator to roll the entire camera left or right.

Undermodulation: an audio signal of little electrical strength.

Vectorscope: a machine used by the Engineer to monitor chrominance levels.

Video Clip Time: the precise duration of a video clip.

Video Monitor: a video viewing device.

Video Program: the final mix of video sources flowing from the video switcher.

Video Server: a PC- and server-based video storage and playback system.

Video Switcher or Vision Mixer: a video selection console operated by the Technical Director.

Video Tape Recorder (VTR): an audio/video playback and recording tape machine.

Viewfinder: a small video monitor located on top of the studio television camera that shows the operator what the camera is seeing.

Vision Mixer (see Technical Director or Video Switcher): UK.

Voice-Over (VO): a story format that features the anchor narrating over video.

Voice-Over Followed by Sound on Tape (VO/SOT): a story format that begins with the anchor narrating over video (VO) immediately followed by an audio cut to a pre-edited sound bite sourced from the tape (SOT).

Volume: a human perception of loudness.

Volume Unit (VU): a measurement scale of audio signal strength.

Wave Form Monitor: a machine used by the Engineer to monitor video luminance levels.

Wheel Lock: a lock located on the pedestal dolly wheel that prevents the wheel from rotating.

White Balance: a procedure used to calibrate the manner in which a camera references color.

Wipe: a video transition that uses an effect to separate the outgoing video source from the incoming video source.

X-Axis: horizontal axis.

XLR Cable: a three-wire audio cable (three-pin).

Y-Axis: vertical axis.

Z-Axis: depth axis.

Zoom: a command cue for the studio Camera Operator to engage the zoom controller (either to "zoom in" or to "zoom out").

Index

178

179

180

CPSIA information can be obtained at www.ICGtesting.com
Printed in the USA
LVOW10s2126120813

347521LV00011B/223/P

9 780240 808734